W9-BXY-567

Private Cuisine

An Executive Chef's Secrets to Gourmet

Cooking Made Easy

David Daniluk

©1999 by David Daniluk

1999 First Edition

ISBN: 0-9673719-0-2

Library of Congress Number: 99-66087

Cover by Denny Wendell

Illustrations by Joyce Klauder

Layout by Francine Smith

Cover Photo: William Gelber
3rd Hole, Radnor Valley Country Club

All rights reserved under all Copyright Conventions.
Submit all requests for reprinting to:
Greenleaf Enterprises, P.O. Box 291, Chesterland, Ohio 44026

Published in the United States by
Greenleaf Enterprises, Inc. Cleveland, Ohio.

http://www.greenleafenterprises.com

I dedicate this book to my loving wife, LENORE, who has always been my true inspiration in cooking and in life.

To my DAD, I only wish you were here. Love you.

In Memory of:

Carol Sankey Jandura
1960-1999

You were a true friend...

xoxoxo

Make-A-Wish Foundation®
of Philadelphia & Southeastern Pennsylvania

Acknowledgements

I would like to thank the following people for their special contributions:

First and foremost, my wife **Lenore** and my two wonderful boys **Joshua** and **Dylan**. Thanks for bearing with me through this. The kids were tired of hearing me say, "I'm working on the book."

Joyce Klauder for her fantastic sketches. My only regret is that I didn't have her do more. Thank you for everything.

My sous chef, **Stephen Szentlaszloi**, for his continued loyalty. I have been fortunate to have you with me all these years.

Clint Greenleaf of Greenleaf Enterprises, Inc. and **Kim Rose** of Data Reproductions. Their help in getting this book up and running was invaluable. I look forward to our next project.

William Gelber of William Gelber Photography for his great cover shot.

The entire membership of **Radnor Valley Country Club** for their continual support over the last ten years.

About the Author

. . . .

As told by Kevin M. Dwyer, General Manager, Radnor Valley Country Club

Where to begin? Executive Chef Daniluk is one of the most talented and artistic individuals in the industry. The creative recipes described in this book are only the tip of the iceberg. I'm sure there will be future editions of Private Cuisine for your enjoyment. As you will realize, this cookbook will enlighten you on some of David's techniques to prepare gourmet foods easily in your home kitchen.

I have had the distinct privilege of working with Chef Daniluk at Radnor Valley Country Club for five years as General Manager. This experience has been nothing short of most rewarding. In the private club industry, the chef is under the constant scrutiny of the membership to provide the finest food in all aspects. David is in the middle of his 10th season at RVCC. This longevity at a private club can be attributed to many of his qualities. David's creativity never ceases to amaze me. His inspirations occur at the oddest of times. It is common for David to create a five-course gourmet dinner menu while driving home from the club after a fourteen-hour day. His genuine concern for quality in preparation and presentation is a major part of his daily focus. The end result is a truly exceptional dining experience.

What makes David extraordinary is that his talents extend beyond the typical responsibilities of a chef. His willingness to provide his guests with the best dining experience really sets him apart. On many occasions, David has taken time to meet with members to discuss their personal dining interests and special events to ensure that their expectations will be exceeded.

Since Chef Daniluk and I originally discussed the concept of Private Cuisine a short two years ago, he has been dedicated to producing a high quality publication to benefit the Make-A-Wish Foundation. I am confident that you will get to know David, particularly his passion for fine food, as you experience his talents outlined in this book.

As we say on all of our menus at the club, "Sit back, relax and enjoy!"

Table of Contents

Introduction

Introduction
· · · · · · · · · · · · · · · · · ·

For as long as I can remember I have wanted to be a chef but felt I needed formal training. I attended college and graduated with a business management degree. I worked in various restaurants throughout high school and college gathering whatever knowledge I could about cooking. I traveled whenever possible, always paying close attention to regional food preparations. I read about anything that had to do with food and still do. In this business you can never know enough and will never know everything.

One day I decided it was time for me to take a chance. I applied at the Frog/Commissary Restaurant in Philadelphia, Pa. for a sous chef position. I interviewed with the executive chef and explained that though I did not have the experience, I had the drive and knowledge to do the job. I left that interview with a job offer for making sandwiches at a piano bar for $4.50/hour. The chef told me that as long as I showed mastery of one position he would move me throughout the restaurant. I accepted that job and it was the best thing I ever did. However, I must say that if it weren't for my wife, I would have never gone to that interview. I also would not have accepted that job but she truly believed in me and said now was the time.

The chef was true to his word. I moved from sandwiches, to salads, to sauces and soups. I learned how to clean fish and break down meats. I worked in the bakery learning to make breads, muffins and pastries. Within two years I was in a chef position in one of the companies restaurants. I also worked supervising parties in their catering department, considered to be one of the cities finest. I was afforded the opportunity to work as a live-in chef for one of their larger catering clients. I spent 5 months serving gourmet meals for 2-100 people. It was an incredible experience. I remember walking in the first day around 4 p.m. The client told me that they would love a soufflé to be served with dinner. I explained that soufflés were not my strong point and was given the answer "Dinner will be served at 6."

I served a great dinner that night, though the caramelized onion soufflé was served after the entrée because I had not timed it right. I spent the summer at the Jersey shore in Margate making homemade jams, canning tomatoes, preserving peaches, making ice creams and serving foods that I had only dreamed of. That time proved to me that I had what it took to be a well-rounded gourmet chef.

In 1990 I came to Radnor Valley Country Club in Villanova, PA for a change of pace. I wanted to see what the club scene was all about. I figured I would try it for about a year to see what it was like. Well, it is 1999 and I am still here and loving it. The club has maintained a small, intimate operation that allows me to continue to cook every night behind the line-which is what I truly love. We change the menu about 8 times a year, always using only the finest seasonal product available. Well, enough about my history and me.

I would like to get to the reason why I have written this book. I have always believed that the key to a good dining experience, aside from good service and atmosphere, is to use a fresh, high quality product. If you do not have the freshest fish or a quality piece of meat, it doesn't matter how you prepare it. I also believe that you can prepare this food in your home. I have tried to customize recipes to make them easier for the home cook. I hope to enlighten you on different foods and why they may be worth a try. I have tried to give you tips on buying fish, meats and seasonal produce. Cooking at home does not have to be so intimidating.

Too often there is an abundance of flavors incorporated into one dish. The true flavor of the dish is compromised. I try not to overpower the main part of a dish, but only complement it. Imagination can be a big part of being a chef, but determining what flavors go together and, more importantly, which flavors don't, is the key. Food is an important part of our lives and it should be enjoyed. I hope that this book helps you to do that. I would finally like to mention another reason for writing this book. I have been blessed with a wonderful family and a good life. Therefore, 100% of the proceeds will be donated to the Make-A-Wish Foundation in hopes of giving a little bit back.

Equipment

*A well-stocked kitchen makes cooking easier and more fun.
The following is a list of items that may just make your next cooking
experience a more pleasurable one.*

Coffee Grinder – Freshly ground spices are far superior in flavor to spices that are already ground. Ground spices are likely to have impurities and fillers. A small, inexpensive coffee grinder is the best way to go.

Blender – This is the best machine for making salad dressings. A food processor works, but the blender emulsifies better.

Food Processor – Invaluable to any kitchen. Great for pureeing soups and sauces. Saves you a lot of time, which you don't always have at home.

Large Sauté Pans – Everyone should have at least one 12 or 14 in. sauté pan. The nonstick surfaces today are far superior to their earlier counterparts. I rarely walk into a home that has a pan this size. You can cook a meal for 4 in a pan that size. It saves time and cleanup.

Squirt Bottles – You can find these in a dollar store. Great for keeping flavored oils, fruit purees or vinaigrettes. You can decorate your plates when entertaining or easily drizzle over a salad. Keep extra sauces in refrigerator for future use.

Juicer – A must for fresh carrot or other vegetable juice. Great for fresh citrus juices.

Outdoor Grill – If possible, don't put away your gas grill after summer. It's wonderful to grill a nice lobster or steak in the middle of winter. You can do your whole meal on the grill for easy cleanup.

Stockpot – A stockpot should be taller than it is wide. A 12 qt. size will leave you room for large bones but will not be too cumbersome to lift.

Food Mill – The best for mashed potatoes. Food is forced through perforated metal disks. There are usually disks with three degrees of coarseness.

Chinois (shin-wah) – This fine wire mesh strainer is used for straining stocks when smooth results are needed.

Knives – If you cook at home, it is worth having a good set of knives. Look for knives with a sturdy construction-the blade of the knife should run inside the handle and be attached with rivets. Keep them sharp with an electric knife sharpener and steel. Use a wooden cutting board, which will lengthen the life of the blade and make chopping easier. An 8 in. chef knife is the easiest to handle and most used. A good paring knife for peeling vegetables is also a must. There are many more knives available for slicing, boning meats and fowl and filleting fish. Purchase the ones that will best suit your needs.

Meat Thermometers – Dial thermometers are inserted into the food and left until the desired temperature is achieved. However, these thermometers may distort cooking times by conducting additional heat to the food center. Instant read thermometers are much more accurate. They may be inserted for about 1 minute while food is in the oven. An instant read thermometer is well worth the $12-20 investment.

Citrus Zester – A small tool that removes the outer layer of citrus without removing the bitter white pith.

Mandoline – This machine has an adjustable blade for slicing, shredding or cutting a julienne. A real time saver, the price range being anywhere from $15-150.

Hors d'oeuvres

When you are searching for the perfect first course to serve to your guests-look no further. This is a stunning presentation that will certainly please.

Grilled Lobster and Mango Cocktail

SERVES 4

4 each-4 oz. Cold water lobster tails
2 T. Olive oil
1 tsp. Shallots-minced
1 T. Fresh basil-chopped
2 ½ C. Fresh mango-diced (2 mangoes)
¼ C. Fresh squeezed orange juice
1 T. Grapeseed oil
Salt & fresh ground pepper to taste
1 T. Red bell pepper-fine diced
2 tsp. Chives-snipped

Split lobster tails down the middle, not cutting all the way through. Remove meat from shells. Score the bottom of each tail with 3 half inch slices. This will keep the tail from curling while grilling. Toss lobster tails with olive oil, shallots and basil. Let marinate up to 8 hours.

Meanwhile in a blender place ½ cup of mangoes and orange juice and blend until smooth. With machine running add grapeseed oil. Remove from bowl and season with salt and pepper. Refrigerate- can be made up to 3 days ahead.

Place lobster tails on a medium high grill and cook for about 3 minutes per side or until cooked through. When cool, cut lobster into 1 in. cubes and toss with remaining mangoes, bell pepper and chives. Refrigerate. When ready to serve, place in chilled martini glasses. Drizzle with mango-orange puree. Garnish with whole fresh chives.

When making the following two recipes you do not need to be concerned with the size of the shrimp. Neither recipe will be using the shrimp whole, but remember, the better quality of shrimp, the better the dish will taste.

Southwestern Shrimp & Corn Fritters

MAKES 16-2 INCH FRITTERS

¾ Lb. Shrimp, deveined & chopped into ½ in. pieces
3 Ears corn, kernels scraped off
1 tsp. Garlic, minced
2 tsp. Ancho chile powder
1 tsp. Ground cumin seed
1 tsp. Ground coriander seed
2 T. Fresh cilantro-chopped
Tabasco to taste
3 ½ T. Flour mixed with ½ tsp. baking powder
3 Eggs, beaten
1 tsp. Salt
Peanut oil for frying

In a mixing bowl combine shrimp, corn, garlic, chile powder, cumin, coriander, cilantro, tabasco, flour mix, eggs and salt. Mix ingredients thoroughly.

Heat a wok and add peanut oil to a depth of 2 inches. Heat oil to 375°. Add shrimp fritters, about 5 at a time, and cook until golden brown, about 2 minutes per side. Remove from oil and drain on paper towels. Keep warm while frying remaining fritters. Serve with your favorite dipping sauce.

Thai Shrimp Toasts

. . . .

YIELDS 8 TOASTS

½ Lb. Raw shrimp, peeled and deveined
2 tsp. Red curry paste
1 T. Ginger-minced
2 tsp. Garlic-minced
2 Egg whites
1 tsp. Sesame oil
1 tsp. Cornstarch
1 T. Soy sauce
2 tsp. Cilantro-chopped
2 T. Shredded coconut
1 T. Sesame seeds
8 - ½ in. Thick slices french bread

Place shrimp, curry paste, ginger, garlic and egg whites in bowl of food processor. Puree mixture until smooth. Add sesame oil, soy sauce and cornstarch and blend into shrimp mixture. Remove mixture from processor. Stir cilantro, coconut, and sesame seeds into shrimp mixture.

In a large skillet, heat about ¾ in. of peanut oil to 350°. Press shrimp mixture onto french bread slices. Carefully immerse toasts, shrimp side down, into hot oil and fry for 3 minutes or until golden brown. Remove from oil and drain on paper towels.

To save a little time, make the crab salad a day ahead. This is a quick appetizer, great for that special dinner party.

Jumbo Lump Crab Crostini

24 - ½ in. Thick slices french bread
3 T. Olive oil
1 T. Old Bay seasoning
1 Lb. Jumbo lump crab-picked over
¾ C. Mayonnaise
2 T. Dijon mustard
1 T. Red pepper-minced
1 T. Red onion-minced
1 T. Chives-snipped
Juice of 2 lemons
Tabasco to taste

Preheat oven to 400°. Toss french bread with olive oil and Old Bay. Spread baguette slices on a baking sheet and cook for about 5 minutes. Remove from oven.

Combine crabmeat, mayonnaise, mustard, red peppers, onion, chives, and lemon juice. Mix well. Season with tabasco.

Spread crab mixture on toasted baguettes. Bake crab crostini in oven for about 10 minutes, or until heated through. Serve immediately.

Crab and Gruyere Stuffed Mushrooms

3 T. Unsalted butter
3 T. Onion-minced
2 T. Red bell pepper-minced
1 T. Dry sherry
½ C. Heavy cream
1 T. Dijon mustard
8 oz. Lump crabmeat-picked of shells
1 T. Parsley-chopped
2 tsp. Chives-snipped
⅛ tsp. Salt
Tabasco to taste
1 T. Fresh lemon juice
2 T. Japanese bread crumbs
⅓ C. Gruyere cheese-shredded
16 Lg. Mushrooms-stems removed & brushed with olive oil

Preheat oven to 375°. Place a medium saucepan over medium high heat and melt butter. Add onions and peppers and sauté for 2-3 minutes. Add dry sherry and cook additional 1 minute. Remove from heat. Stir in heavy cream, dijon mustard, crabmeat, parsley, chives, salt, tabasco, lemon juice and bread crumbs. Mix thoroughly, being careful not to break up crabmeat. Sprinkle with gruyere cheese. Bake in oven for 10-15 minutes until hot and cheese is lightly browned.

Oysters with Chile Mignonette

FOR 24 OYSTERS

24- Freshly shucked oysters
1 T. Shallots-minced
2 tsp. Red bell pepper-minced
2 tsp. Yellow bell pepper-minced
2 tsp. Poblano pepper-minced
1 tsp. Jalapeno pepper-minced
1 T. Cilantro-chopped
2 T. Fresh lime juice
½ tsp. Ancho chile powder

Chill oysters. Toss remaining ingredients together and refrigerate for 1 hour. Top each oyster with ½ tsp. of mignonette and serve.

This is one of my wife Lenores' favorite treats. It is also one of mine, but unfortunately I am allergic to oysters.

Pecan Fried Oysters with Lemon Caper Mayonnaise

. . . .

¾ C. Panko crumbs
¼ C. Fine breadcrumbs
½ C. Pecans-fine chopped
1 tsp. Old Bay
Salt and fresh ground pepper to taste
4 Large eggs-beaten
24 Jumbo oysters-freshly shucked and patted dry
½ C. Vegetable oil for frying

Mix panko crumbs, fine breadcrumbs, pecans, Old Bay and salt and pepper. Dip oysters, a few at a time, in egg, then roll in pecan-breadcrumb mixture.

Heat oil in a heavy bottomed fry pan. Fry oysters, a few at a time, for about 30 seconds on each side, or until golden brown. Drain on paper towels. Serve oysters with lemon caper mayonnaise.

Lemon Caper Mayonnaise

. . . .

MAKES ¾ CUP

¾ C. Mayonnaise
1 T. Fresh squeezed lemon juice
2 T. Capers-minced
1 T. Parsley-chopped
1 tsp. Snipped chives
Tabasco sauce to taste

Combine all ingredients and mix well. Can be prepared a day in advance.

Tired of eating those same old buffalo style chicken wings?
Try this recipe next time and you may never go back.

Oriental Black Bean BBQ Chicken Wings

SERVES 4-6

½ C. Ketchup
½ C. Molasses
½ C. Soy sauce
¼ C. Chili sauce
¼ C. Honey
¼ C. Brown sugar
* ¼ C. fermented black beans (rinsed in cold water, then chopped)
1 T. Ginger-minced
1 T. Garlic-minced
* 3 T. Sriracha-asian hot sauce
2 T. Sesame seeds
3 Lb. Chicken wings-disjointed

* Available in oriental markets

In a large mixing bowl combine all ingredients except chicken wings. Mix thoroughly. Toss in chicken wings and let marinate for a least 4 hours.

Place chicken wings on a baking sheet in a single layer. Bake at 400° for 35-45 minutes, stirring around once or twice during that time to ensure even cooking. Barbecue sauce will give the wings a nice caramelized glaze. You will save yourself a mess if you line your baking sheet with heavy-duty aluminum foil.

If you don't have a grill available, bake in a preheated 375° oven for 5-6 minutes. You can prepare these brochettes well ahead of time. Just freeze uncooked chicken brochettes on a flat baking pan. Remove chicken from freezer the night before and you will be ready to go.

Grilled Chicken Brochettes with Pickled Cucumber Relish

· · · · · · · · · · · · · · · · · · · ·

SERVES 4

1 Lb. boneless, skinless chicken breast-cut into 1 inch cubes
1 T. Fresh ginger-minced
2 tsp. Fresh garlic-minced
2 T. Honey
¼ C. Fresh lime juice
2 tsp. Sriracha

Toss chicken with ginger, garlic, honey, lime juice and sriracha. Let marinate for about 30 minutes, tossing occasionally. Place chicken cubes on wooden skewers. Grill over medium heat for 3-4 minutes per side. Serve with cucumber relish.

Pickled Cucumber Relish

· · · · · · · · · · · · · · · · · · · ·

1 ½ C. cucumber, peeled, seeded and diced
3 T. Rice wine vinegar
2 tsp. Pickled ginger-minced
2 T. Cilantro-chopped
1 T. Red bell pepper-minced
2 tsp. Jalapeno pepper-minced

Toss all ingredients together and let marinate for at least 30 minutes and up to 3 hours.

Marinated Chevre

¼ C. Extra virgin olive oil
1 T. Garlic-minced
¼ tsp. Red pepper flakes
⅓ C. Kalamata olives-pitted & halved
1 tsp. Fresh thyme leaves
1 tsp. Fresh rosemary
1 T. Fresh basil-chopped
1-11 oz. Chevre log

Place a small sauté pan over medium heat. Add olive oil, garlic and red pepper flakes and simmer for 1 minute. Add olives and cook additional 2 minutes. Remove from heat and let cool. Add thyme, rosemary and basil.

Carefully slice chevre into 1 in. slices. Place slices in a flat-bottomed casserole. Pour olive-herb mixture over chevre and refrigerate. Let marinate up to 36 hours.

Serve with sliced tomatoes, in a salad, or with french bread.

Macadamia Nut Baked Brie

SERVES 20

Kilo wheel of brie
1 ½ C. Macadamia nuts-chopped fine
Sliced apples & french bread for garnish

Carefully cut rind from top of Brie, being careful not to cut rind from sides. The sides are needed to form a wall for the warm cheese. Spread nuts evenly over the top of the cheese. Cheese can be prepared to this point up to 2 days ahead. Bring cheese to room temperature. Place cheese on a foil lined baking sheet sprayed with non-stick cooking spray. Place cheese at least 6 in. under preheated broiler. Broil for 1-2 minutes or until nuts are evenly browned. Be careful not to overcook. Carefully lift cheese to serving platter and remove foil. Serve garnished with sliced apples and french bread.

There is a nice variety of flavored tortillas in most supermarket refrigerator and freezer sections. I like to use two different flavored tortillas when serving this hors d'oeuvre; the two colors give a little added effect in presentation. These can be made up to a day ahead of time.

Smoked Salmon and Avocado Rolls

. . . .

MAKES ABOUT 28 PIECES

1 C. Avocado-cored, peeled and diced
2 T. Fresh squeezed lemon juice
1 tsp. Ground cumin
2 tsp. Fresh cilantro-chopped
¼ tsp. Salt
Ground black pepper to taste
4 - 8 in. Flour tortillas-any flavored variety
1 Lb. Thinly sliced smoked salmon
½ C. Fresh tomatoes-peeled, seeded, finely diced
2 T. Fresh chives-snipped

In a food processor puree avocado, lemon juice and cumin. Stir in cilantro, salt and pepper. Spread avocado puree on tortillas, covering completely. Lay sliced salmon over avocado puree, leaving a ½ in. border on one side of the tortilla. Sprinkle with diced tomatoe. Starting from end covered with salmon, roll tortilla up tightly. Slice ½ in. off one end of tortilla roll. Slice 1 in. thick pinwheels, about 7 to a tortilla. Garnish with snipped chives.

Grilled Eggplant and Chevre Bruschetta

2 Medium eggplant-peeled and cut into ¾ in. slices
2 T. Kosher salt
¼ C. Olive oil mixed with ¼ C. balsamic vinegar
24 - ¾ in. Thick slices french baguette
2 T. Fresh garlic-minced
¼ C. Olive oil
8 oz. Chevre-crumbled
¼ C. Sundried tomatoes, chopped (softened in hot water)
2 T. Fresh basil-chopped

Place eggplant in a large colander and sprinkle with salt. Place in sink or over a bowl and let sit for 1 hour. This will remove any bitter juices eggplant may have.

Remove eggplant slices from colander, wiping away any excess moisture and salt. Brush each eggplant slice with oil and vinegar mixture. Grill over high heat for 2 minutes on each side. Remove from grill and cover with aluminum foil.

Toss bread with garlic and olive oil. Bake in a 400° oven for about 5 minutes or until slightly crisp.

Uncover eggplant and chop into a small dice. In a mixing bowl, toss eggplant with chevre, sundried tomatoes and basil.

It will have the consistency of a spread. Top each baguette with eggplant spread. Drizzle with remaining oil & vinegar mixture. Serve.

Herbed Cream Cheese Spread

1 Lb. Cream cheese
¼ C. Sour cream
1 T. Minced garlic
1 T. Fresh dill-chopped
1 T. Fresh basil-chopped
Salt and pepper to taste

Place cream cheese, sour cream, garlic, dill and basil in an electric mixing bowl. Mix on high for 2 minutes. Scrape down sides and mix another 2 minutes. Season with salt & pepper. Wonderful dip for fresh vegetables, crackers, or french bread. Low fat or non-fat cream cheese can be substituted.

Tomato Green Chile Salsa

MAKES 4 CUPS

2 C. Crushed tomatoes (good quality)
1 C. Fresh tomato-peeled, seeded & diced
½ C. Roasted green chiles-diced (fresh or canned)
1 T. Fresh squeezed lime juice
1 T. Cilantro-chopped
2 T. Red onion-minced
1 tsp. Ground cumin seed
1 tsp. Ground coriander seed
1 tsp. Ground ancho chiles
1 T. Red bell pepper-minced
1 T. Yellow bell pepper-minced
Salt & fresh ground pepper to taste

Mix all ingredients in a bowl and let stand in refrigerator for about 2 hours. Use as needed. Salsa will last up to a week in refrigerator.

Guacamole

6 C. avocado (about 3 or 4 avocados)-peeled, cored and diced
4 T. Lime juice
¼ C. Red onion-chopped
1 Jalapeno pepper-seeded and chopped
3 T. Fresh cilantro-chopped
2 tsp. Fresh ground ancho chili powder
2 tsp. Fresh ground cumin seed
1 tsp. Salt
1 ½ C. Fresh tomatoes-diced

In a food processor puree 3 C. of the avocado, 2 T. lime juice, red onion and jalapeno pepper until smooth.

Toss remaining 2 T. lime juice with remaining 3 C. avocado to prevent discoloration.

Place puree in a mixing bowl and add diced avocado, cilantro, chili powder, cumin seed, salt and diced tomatoes. Mix well. Serve with tortilla chips or fat free pita chips.

Instead of putting out plain old nuts, try one of these recipes for your next party. You can substitute walnuts for either of these recipes. They can also be made days ahead, if time is a factor.

Ancho Chile Roasted Cashews

YIELD 4 CUPS

1 T. Peanut oil
2 tsp. Ancho chile powder
½ tsp. Pasilla chile powder
1 tsp. Ground cumin
1 tsp. Ground coriander
1 tsp. Kosher salt
3 T. Honey
4 C. Unsalted cashews

Preheat oven to 325°. Place cashews in a mixing bowl. Toss cashews with oil, chile powders, cumin, coriander, salt and honey. Mix thoroughly to coat nuts evenly. Spread nuts in a single layer on a baking sheet sprayed with non-stick cooking spray. Bake cashews for 10-12 minutes, stirring once during that time, until nuts are golden brown. Serve as a snack or in a salad. Store in an airtight container.

Honey Caramelized Pecans

2 C. Shelled pecans (walnuts can be substituted)
½ C. Honey
1 tsp. Ground coriander seed
1 tsp. Ground cumin seed
½ tsp. Paprika
¼ tsp. Cayenne pepper
1 tsp. Kosher salt

Preheat oven to 375°. Toss nuts with honey and all the spices. Spread nuts on a baking sheet sprayed with non-stick cooking spray. Bake for 8-10 minutes until nuts are a nice golden brown. Stir pecans once during this time. Remove nuts from oven and let cool. Break nuts apart and place in an airtight container. Nuts will last up to 3 weeks. Great in salads or as a snack.

Roasted Eggplant and Red Pepper Dip

3 Eggplants-about ½ lb. each, brushed with olive oil
3 Red peppers (roasted, peeled and seeded)
3 Garlic cloves
½ C. Tahini
1 T. Lemon juice
1 each Jalapeno pepper (seeded & finely diced)
¼ C. Olive oil
Salt & pepper to taste

Preheat oven to 400°. Roast eggplant, covered with foil, for about 35 minutes or until soft. When slightly cooled, peel eggplant and place pulp in food processor with roasted peppers, garlic, tahini, lemon juice and jalapeno pepper. Puree eggplant mixture until smooth. With machine running, slowly add olive oil. Season with salt & pepper. Serve with pita crisps.

Roasted Red Pepper & Black Olive Hummus

2 C. Garbonzo beans-drained
⅓ C. Tahini (sesame seed paste)
¼ C. Water
3 T. Fresh lemon juice
3 Garlic cloves
½ C. Roasted peppers (see recipe)
¼ C. Pitted calamata olives-chopped
¼ tsp. Salt
1 tsp. Tabasco
3 T. Chopped parsley
¼ C. Olive oil

In a food processor blend together garbonzo beans, tahini, water, lemon juice and garlic. Blend until mixture is smooth.

Add roasted peppers, olives, salt, tabasco, parsley and olive oil.

Blend until ingredients are fully incorporated. If too thick, add more water. Great dip for pita chips or fresh vegetables.

Stocks and Soups

Stocks

. . . .

    I realize that stocks are probably one of the least prepared items of the home cook. However, whenever you have time you can make stocks and freeze them in containers for future use. I also never miss the opportunity to make stock with a leftover cooked chicken or turkey carcass. There are a few things to remember whenever making stocks. You do not want a stock to boil rapidly for more than a minute or two (unless you're making veal stock for demiglace). The boiling will cause the stock to cloud. Also, be sure to skim off any of the foaming impurities that come to the surface of the stock while it is simmering. It is also always a good idea to let stocks cool completely before using, as this allows any fat to accumulate at the top of the stock. If time is a factor, you can carefully skim off as much fat as possible with a ladle. You can then gently skim the top of the stock with a sturdy, absorbent paper towel to absorb any remaining fat. I know that stocks can be time consuming but, homemade stocks simply make better soups and sauces than bouillon cubes or canned stocks.

Lobster Stock

. . . .

MAKES 4 QUARTS

3 Lb. Lobster shells
1 C. Dry white wine
2 Onions-halved
1 Celery stalk
2 Bay leaf
2 tsp. Dried thyme
10 Black peppercorns
2 C. Diced tomatoes
10 qts. Water

    Place lobster shells in a roasting pan. Roast in a 425° oven for 35 minutes. Scrape shells into a large stockpot. Deglaze roasting pan with white wine. Scrape bottom of pan, pouring wine into stockpot. Add remaining ingredients to stockpot. Bring stock to a boil, then reduce to a simmer. Cook stock for 4-5 hours. Stock will be reduced by half. Strain stock through a fine sieve. Taste stock. If a richer stock is desired, place into a clean stockpot and reduce until desired richness. Stock freezes well.

This is just one version of vegetable stock. You can save trimmings from any number of vegetables to use for stock. If you don't have enough trimmings, you can throw them in a ziplock bag, freeze and use at a later time.

Vegetable Stock

MAKES ABOUT 4 QUARTS

2 T. Olive oil
2 Onions-rough chopped
3 Carrots-rough chopped
1 Bulb fennel-rough chopped
2 Celery stalks-rough chopped
2 T. Tomato paste
½ C. Dry sherry
1 Head garlic-halved
4 Shallots-halved
2 C. Diced tomato in juice
2 T. Balsamic vinegar
6 qts. Water
5 Sprigs Fresh thyme
5 Sprigs Fresh parsley
10 Black peppercorns
Salt to taste

In a large stockpot heat olive oil. Add onions, carrots, fennel and celery. Sauté vegetables for about 10 minutes, lightly browning them. Add tomato paste and sherry and cook additional 2 minutes.

Add garlic, shallots, diced tomatoes, vinegar, water, thyme, parsley and peppercorns. Bring stock to a boil, then reduce to a simmer and cook for 1 ½ hours. Strain stock through a fine sieve and season with salt to taste. This stock freezes well.

Basic Chicken Stock
· · · · · · · · · · · · · · · · · · · ·
MAKES ABOUT 3 ½ QUARTS

1 T. Olive oil
5 Lb. Chicken backs or carcasses
2 Carrots-rough chopped
2 Whole onions-halved
2 Celery stalks-rough chopped
4 Garlic cloves-halved
5 Sprigs Fresh thyme or 1 tsp. dried thyme
3 Sprigs Fresh parsley
2 Bay leaves
10 Black peppercorns
10 qts. Water

Heat a large stockpot and add olive oil. Add chicken bones and brown for about 5 minutes. Add carrots, onion, celery, garlic, thyme, parsley, bay leaves, peppercorns and water. Bring stock to a boil and skim any foam that comes to top. Reduce to a simmer and cook for 3-4 hours. Strain stock through a fine sieve or cheesecloth. Cool and refrigerate. Skim off any fat from the surface of the chilled stock. Refrigerate up to 5 days, freeze up to 6 months.

Brown Chicken Stock

5 Lb. Chicken backs or carcasses
¼ C. Dry white wine
1 T. Olive oil
2 Carrots-rough chopped
2 Whole onions-rough chopped
2 Celery stalks-rough chopped
4 Garlic cloves-halved
5 Sprigs thyme
3 Sprigs parsley
2 Bay leaf
10 Black peppercorns
10 qts. Water

Place bones in a roasting pan and cook in a 400° oven for 40 minutes. Remove pan from oven and drain off accumulated fat. Meanwhile heat a 12 qt. stockpot and add olive oil. Add carrots, onion, celery, and garlic to pan. Sauté for 15 minutes, stirring occasionally to brown vegetables. Add roasted chicken bones to pot. Place roasting pan on stovetop burners and deglaze with white wine. Scrape bottom of pan to release any brown bits. Pour into stockpot and add thyme, parsley, bay leaf, peppercorns and water. Bring stock to a boil and remove any foam that comes to the top. Reduce to a simmer and cook for 5-6 hours. Add water as needed. Strain stock and let stand for 10 minutes. Skim fat off top. Return to stockpot and reduce stock for about 1 hour. You should have about 1 ½ qts. Stock freezes very well.

Basic Veal Stock

MAKES 4 QUARTS

10 Lb. Veal bones
4 Onions-halved
3 Carrots-rough chopped
3 Celery stalks-rough chopped
6 Garlic cloves-halved
2 C. Burgundy
1 C. Tomato paste
8 qts. Water
8 Sprigs Fresh thyme
6 Sprigs Parsley
4 Bay leaf
10 Black peppercorns

Place veal bones in a roasting pan. Roast at 400° for 1 ½ hours. Add carrots, onions, celery and garlic and cook additional 15 minutes. Remove from oven and pour bones and vegetables into large stockpot. Place roasting pan on stovetop over high heat. Add burgundy and tomato paste and scrape bottom of pan to release the flavors from the pan. Pour wine mixture into stockpot with veal bones and cover with 4 qts. water. Bring stock to a boil and skim off any foam. Reduce heat to a simmer for 10-12 hours. Strain stock through a fine sieve and let cool. Refrigerate, then remove layer of condensed fat. Refrigerate up to 5 days or freeze up to 6 months.

I realize making veal demiglace can be daunting for the home chef. However, it is wonderful for steaks, chicken, lamb, and once made will go a long way.

Veal Demiglace

1 ½ QUARTS

Place 4 qts. of veal stock into a stockpot. Reduce veal stock over medium heat until reduced by a little more than half. Strain stock through a fine sieve. This will give you a rich meat sauce. I will refer to this recipe throughout the book. Demiglace can be frozen in ice cube trays, then removed and placed in a ziplock freezer bag. Remove as many as you need for a recipe.

Tomato Avocado Gazpacho

. . . .

MAKES ABOUT 8 CUPS

2 Large, ripe tomatoes-peeled, seeded & diced
¼ C. Red bell pepper, seeded and finely diced
¼ C. Yellow bell pepper, seeded and finely diced
¼ C. Poblano pepper, seeded and finely diced
¼ C. Red onion, finely diced
¼ C. Fresh squeezed lime juice
4 C. Crushed tomatoes (good quality canned product)
1 tsp. Fresh garlic, minced
3 C. Cucumber, peeled, seeded and diced
½ C. Ice water
2 T. Fresh chopped cilantro
2 tsp. Fresh ground cumin seed
1 tsp. Fresh ground coriander seed
* 2 tsp. Fresh ground ancho chiles
Salt & fresh ground pepper to taste
2 Avocado (peeled, seeded & diced) best done when serving, as avocado will
discolor rapidly

* *If dried ancho chile peppers are not available, substitute 1 tsp. ground chile powder*

In a large bowl mix diced tomatoes, red, yellow and poblano peppers, red onion, lime juice, crushed tomatoes, garlic and 1 ½ cups cucumber.

In a food processor or blender puree remaining 1 ½ cups cucumber and ice water until smooth.

Add pureed cucumber to tomato mixture and season with cilantro, ground cumin, coriander, and ancho chile powder. Add salt and fresh ground pepper to taste.

Chill, and when serving, top each portion with diced avocado.

Serve either of these chilled soups on a hot summer day as a stunning first course or a wonderfully different dessert. A variation on the mango soup as a first course-add a few teaspoons of minced jalapeno peppers to give it a zip.

Chilled Strawberry Peach Soup

2 C. Fresh strawberries, stemmed and halved
2 peaches-peeled, pitted and sliced
1 C. Cottage cheese
3 T. Honey
2 tsp. Fresh squeezed lemon juice
1 C. Heavy cream
Thin sliced strawberries and mint sprigs for garnish

In food processor puree strawberries, peaches, cottage cheese, honey and lemon juice until very smooth. Remove from processor and pour into bowl. Stir in heavy cream and refrigerate until chilled thoroughly. Spoon soup into chilled martini glasses and garnish with strawberries and fresh mint sprig.

Mango Buttermilk Soup

MAKES ABOUT 8 CUPS

4 Large mangoes-very ripe
2 Lb. Navel oranges
3 T. Honey
1 ½ C. Fresh squeezed orange juice
2 C. Buttermilk
½ C. Heavy cream
2 tsp. Fresh mint-chopped

Peel mangoes and remove all flesh from pit. Place mangoes in a blender. With a sharp knife remove peel and the white pith from oranges. Cut oranges into a rough chop and place in blender with mangoes. Add honey and blend mixture on high. Slowly add orange juice to blender and continue mixing until very smooth. Remove from blender and stir in buttermilk, heavy cream and fresh mint. Chill soup thoroughly before serving. Garnish with fresh mint sprig.

Chilled Cucumber Soup

· · · · · · · · · · · · · · · · · · ·

MAKES ABOUT 4 CUPS

4 C. Cucumbers, peeled, seeded and diced
1 C. Yogurt
½ C. Heavy cream
2 T. Fresh dill, chopped
1 ½ T. Red bell pepper-finely diced
1 ½ T. Red onion-finely diced
1 T. Yellow pepper-finely diced
1 tsp. Tabasco
Salt & pepper to taste

In a food processor puree 3 cups of cucumbers with yogurt until smooth. Add heavy cream and incorporate into cucumber puree. Remove from processor and stir in dill, red pepper, red onion, yellow pepper and remaining 1 cup cucumber. Season with tabasco, salt and pepper.

This is a great alternative to your basic split pea. Green split peas can be substituted if yellows are not available.

Yellow Split Pea Soup
with Proscuitto & Gorgonzola

MAKES ABOUT 10 CUPS

1 T. Olive oil
1 T. Garlic-minced
1 C. Onion-diced
1 C. Carrots-fine diced
1 C. Celery-fine diced
½ C. Dry white wine
7 C. Chicken stock (more if needed)
2 C. Yellow split peas
2 tsp. Ground cumin seed
2 tsp. Ground coriander seed
1 tsp. Salt
Fresh ground black pepper to taste
5 thin slices Proscuitto
Crumbled gorgonzola for garnish

Heat olive oil in a heavy-bottomed stockpot. Add garlic, onion, carrot and celery and sauté for about 7 minutes, stirring occasionally. Add white wine and cook additional 1 minute. Add chicken stock, cumin, coriander and split peas and bring mixture to a boil. Reduce to a simmer, and cook until peas are tender-about 1 ½ hours. Season with salt and pepper. If too thick, add additional stock.

For garnish-place proscuitto on a baking sheet. Cook in a 400° oven until very crisp. When cooled, crumble into small pieces. Serve soup topped with crisp proscuitto and crumbled gorgonzola.

If you want to dress this up for a truly fantastic first course-garnish top of each bowl with grilled jumbo shrimp and toasted pumpkin seeds.

Roasted Butternut Squash Bisque

. . . .

MAKES ABOUT 9 CUPS

3 Butternut squash-about 5 cups pureed
3 T. Unsalted butter
1 C. Onion-diced
1 T. Ginger-minced
2 tsp. Shallots-minced
¼ C. Dry sherry
3 C. Chicken stock
1 tsp. Ground cumin seed
1 tsp. Ground coriander seed
½ tsp. Salt
¼ tsp. White pepper
1 C. Heavy cream

Cut squash in half lengthwise and scoop out seeds. Brush outside with olive oil and place on baking sheet cut side down. Bake in oven at 375° for 40 minutes or until very soft. Let cool. Carefully scrape flesh from skin and place in food processor. Process until very smooth. Set aside.

Place a 4 qt. Dutch oven over medium high heat and melt butter. Add onions, ginger and shallots and sauté for 5 minutes, stirring occasionally. Add dry sherry and cook additional 3 minutes. Add chicken stock, cumin, coriander, salt and pepper. Bring to a boil. Reduce heat and whisk in butternut squash puree. Heat through and add heavy cream. Simmer for 5 minutes. Season with additional salt & pepper if needed. If you like thinner soup, add additional chicken stock.

If you don't have dried porcinis, you can substitute another dried mushroom. I prefer porcinis for the rich flavor they impart on the soup. Look for shiitake, crimini, oyster and portabello mushrooms for your sliced assortment.

Wild Mushroom Barley Soup
. . . .
4 QUARTS

2 T. Grapeseed oil
1 C. Onions-diced
1 C. Carrots-diced
1 C. Celery-diced
1 T. Garlic-minced
¼ C. Dry sherry
4 C. Assorted wild mushrooms-sliced
2 T. Dried porcinis-soaked in 1 cup hot water
3 qts Chicken stock
¼ C. Soy sauce
2 T. Worcestershire sauce
1 C. Pearl barley
2 tsp. Dried thyme
¼ tsp. Salt
½ tsp. Black pepper

In an 8 qt. stockpot heat grapeseed oil. Add onion, carrot, celery and garlic and sauté for 5 minutes. Deglaze pan with sherry. Add wild mushrooms and cook an additional 5 minutes until soft. Remove porcinis from hot water, reserving liquid. Chop porcinis very finely. Add porcinis, reserved soaking liquid, chicken stock, soy sauce and worcestershire sauce. Bring to a boil and add barley, thyme, salt and pepper. Bring back to a simmer and cook for about 45 minutes or until barley is soft. Soup freezes well.

Dressings and Flavored Oils

Dressings & Flavored Oils

· · · · · · · · · · · · · · · · · ·

There are many different types of greens available in today's market. When you're making a salad dressing, be sure to take into account what you are using it for. Certain lettuces need more of a zip than others. Taste your dressing with a component of your salad to see if you need more flavor. You may need to add additional vinegar, a squeeze of lemon or salt and pepper. The salad dressings that I make have less oil than most, I prefer an acidic dressing. They are wonderful on salads, as well as grilled chicken or fish. When it comes to salad dressings, everybody has different tastes.

Flavored oils-these are my favorite things to do. I only listed a few, but the possibilities are unlimited. I keep my flavored oils in squirt bottles in the refrigerator. This makes them very handy and extends the life of the oil. When making flavored oils, stick with olive or grapeseed oils. Extra virgin and virgin olive oils tend to overpower the flavor you are trying to create. Grapeseed is a very mild oil that lends itself well to flavoring. Use these oils on baked potatoes, grilled french bread or even a morning bagel. They are also wonderful drizzled over your favorite fish. One note-try to prepare your oils in advance. A little extra time helps the oil gain its full flavor.

Olive Oil

I would just like to explain the different types of olive oils available. It can be confusing. Olive oil is graded by the method of extraction and the resulting acid content of the oil. Virgin oils are extracted from the initial pressing of the olive. Extra virgin is the finest, with an acid content of 1%. Following that is "superfine" at 1.5%, "fine" at 3% and "virgin" at 4%. Pure olive oils are then extracted through a heating process. These are considered 100% olive oil but you will find varying degrees of flavors amongst brands. Pomace oil is then extracted through heating and pressing. This is a rather inferior olive oil and is the least expensive out there. I don't even recommend using it. As I mentioned, there are a lot of brands out there, try different ones and you're sure to find a favorite.

Balsamic Vinegar

This fragrant vinegar is made from the juice of trebbiano grapes. The juice is heated and aged in wooden barrels. Natural evaporation concentrates the flavor. Most of the balsamic vinegar sold in the United States is not aged this way (the label must read Aceto balsamic tradizionale). These varieties lack the flavor and body of the well aged balsamic vinegars, but still impart a unique balance of sweet and sour.

Herbs and Spices

If at all possible, I highly recommend growing your own fresh herbs. Depending on where you live many will withstand the cold winter months to bloom again in the spring (i.e. rosemary, thyme, sage, chives and oregano). I have been successful growing herbs close to my house and covering them with leaves for added protection in the winter. If growing herbs, be sure to pick before flowering, since the plants energy will go to producing flowers and not fragrant leaves. If you nip the buds before blooming, the plant will continue to produce leaves. If growing herbs isn't your thing, supermarkets are consistently carrying a much wider variation of fresh herbs throughout the year.

As I had mentioned earlier, try to buy whole spices whenever possible and grind as needed. Whole spices are far superior in flavor. Keep in sealed containers and away from sunlight to optimize flavor and life of spice.

Salt

I truly believe you cannot cook without it. But, as with most things, moderation is the key. Salt is not all the same. Common table salt is virtually void of any minerals. An additive is used to prevent the salt from caking. Also, a large percentage of the table salt has potassium iodide added (thus the name Iodized salt). Kosher salt is readily available and is the one I prefer to table salt. It has a purer taste and its coarse texture makes it much easier to sprinkle. It also contains no additives. There are also more exotic salts available in today's gourmet markets. My favorite and the one I use quite often at the restaurant and home is fleur de sel (flower of salt). It has actually become more of a staple than kosher salt in our kitchen. This salt is harvested from the salt marshes in France, simply skimmed from the surface and drained off. It is a great finish to grilled meats, vegetables and baked potatoes. If there is one thing I recommend to every home cook, it is to keep a pouch of this fragrant sea salt in your pantry.

Pepper

Pepper should always be freshly ground. Buy whole peppercorns and grind them as needed. Black, white and green peppercorns are the berries of one plant. Black peppercorns are the unripe berries that have been left to dry and darken. White peppercorns are the same berries, ripened with the outer casing removed. Then they are dried giving the peppercorn less heat. Green peppercorns are the unripe berries. They are usually freeze dried or preserved in brine. These peppercorns are very good with poultry or used in cream sauces.

Citrus Oil

Juice of 2 oranges
Juice of 2 lemons
Juice of 2 limes
1 C. Grapeseed oil

Place ingredients in a food processor or blender and puree for 30 seconds. Place in a small saucepan and simmer for about 10 minutes. Strain oil through a fine sieve or cheesecloth. Store in refrigerator for up to 1 month. Wonderful on grilled chicken, fish or lobster.

Roasted Garlic Olive Oil

2 Heads Garlic-brushed with oil
2 C. Olive oil
Salt to taste

Wrap garlic in foil and roast in a 400° oven for about 45 minutes or until soft. Let cool, cut off very top of garlic. Squeeze out flesh of garlic. Place in a food processor or blender with olive oil. Puree until smooth. Place in small saucepan. Place over low heat for about 1 hour. Strain through a fine sieve or cheesecloth. Season with salt. Refrigerate oil for a longer shelf life. Try it on baked potatoes, pasta or french bread.

Fresh Herb Oil

3 T. Fresh Basil
2 T. Fresh chives
2 T. Fresh tarragon
2 T. Fresh parsley
1 T. Fresh garlic-chopped
2 C. Olive oil or grapeseed oil

Place herbs, garlic and oil in food processor or blender. Puree for about 1 minute. Let oil stand for 2 hours. Strain through cheesecloth or fine sieve. Season with salt. Keep refrigerated up to 2 months. Try it on baked or mashed potatoes, pastas or grilled fish.

This gives your salad a great, smoky flavor. But don't delegate this vinaigrette to salads only. It's fantastic on grilled fish, chicken or steak.

Char Grilled Tomato Vinaigrette

MAKES 2 CUPS

6 Plum tomatoes-halved lengthwise and brushed with olive oil
½ C. Balsamic vinegar
2 tsp. Fresh garlic-minced
½ C. Extra virgin olive oil
1 T. Fresh basil-chopped
1 T. Flat leaf parsley-chopped
Salt & pepper to taste

Grill tomatoes over medium heat for about 3 minutes on each side or until lightly charred. Place tomatoes on a plate and cover with foil. When tomatoes have cooled, peel skin and remove seeds. Chop tomatoes into a fine dice and place in a mixing bowl. Add balsamic vinegar and fresh garlic. Whisk in olive oil slowly, pouring in a steady stream, until dressing is emulsified. Stir in basil and parsley. Season with salt and fresh ground black pepper.

Caramelized Red Onion Vinaigrette

MAKES ABOUT 1 ¼ CUP

2 T. Unsalted butter
1 C. Red onion-diced
2 tsp. Fresh garlic-minced
½ C. Balsamic vinegar
¼ C. Cider vinegar
2 T. Dry sherry
1 T. Worcestershire sauce
1 T. Fresh thyme leaves
½ C. Olive oil
Salt and fresh ground pepper to taste

In a medium sauté pan melt butter over medium high heat. Add red onions and garlic and sauté for 6-8 minutes, stirring occasionally, until lightly browned or caramelized. Add balsamic vinegar, cider vinegar, worcestershire and sherry. Reduce mixture by half. Remove from heat and cool. Place onion mixture in a mixing bowl. Add thyme and slowly whisk in olive oil. Season with salt and pepper. Serve dressing at room temperature.

Toasted Walnut Vinaigrette

MAKES ABOUT 1 ¾ CUP

2 T. Dijon mustard
2 T. Honey
⅓ C. Red wine vinegar
½ tsp. Salt
¼ tsp. Fresh ground black pepper
1 tsp. Dried thyme
1 T. Fresh tarragon-chopped
⅓ C. Walnut oil
⅓ C. Grapeseed oil
½ C. Toasted walnuts, chopped

In a mixing bowl combine mustard, honey, red wine vinegar, salt, pepper, thyme and tarragon. Mix well. Slowly whisk in walnut and grapeseed oils until dressing is emulsified. Stir in toasted walnuts. Dressing will keep for 3-5 days.

Sundried Tomato Vinaigrette

MAKES ABOUT 2 CUPS

1 T. & ½ Cup Olive oil
2 T. Garlic-minced
⅓ C. Onions-fine dice
2 tsp. White wine
½ C. Balsamic vinegar
1 C. Crushed tomatoes (good quality canned)
½ C. Sundried tomatoes-chopped & softened in hot water
2 T. Fresh basil-chopped
1 T. Fresh parsley-chopped
1 tsp. Dried oregano
1 tsp. Dried thyme
1 tsp. Salt
½ tsp. Fresh ground black pepper

In a small sauté pan heat 1 T. olive oil. Add onions and garlic and sauté for about 2 minutes. Add white wine and balsamic vinegar and reduce for an additional 2 minutes. Remove from heat and pour mixture into mixing bowl. Add crushed tomatoes, sundried tomatoes, basil, parsley, thyme, salt and pepper. Whisk in remaining ½ cup olive oil. Can be kept in refrigerator for 1 week. This dressing can be made with less olive oil, just add more balsamic vinegar to heighten taste.

Dijon Mustard-Balsamic Vinaigrette

2 CUP YIELD

4 T. Dijon mustard
1 T. Coarse mustard
2 T. Honey
2 tsp. Shallots-minced
½ C. Balsamic vinegar
1 C. Olive oil
Salt & fresh ground black pepper to taste

In a blender combine dijon mustard, coarse mustard, honey and shallots. Mix well. Add in balsamic vinegar with blender on high. Slowly pour olive oil in a steady stream until dressing is emulsified. Season with salt & pepper.

Roasted Garlic Vinaigrette

MAKES ABOUT 2 CUPS

3 Heads garlic, left whole, brushed with olive oil
2 T. Dijon mustard
½ C. Balsamic vinegar
1 T. Fresh lemon juice
1 tsp. Fresh thyme leaves
1 ½ C. Olive oil
Salt & pepper to taste

Wrap garlic heads in foil and roast in a 400° oven for 45 minutes or until garlic is very soft. Let garlic cool, and with a very sharp knife, cut off very top of garlic heads. Squeeze roasted garlic from heads, picking out any skin that may come with it. In a blender mix garlic, mustard, vinegar, lemon juice and thyme leaves until smooth. With machine on, slowly add olive oil into garlic mixture and blend until emulsified. Can be made ahead and refrigerated. Try this drizzled over grilled chicken or fish.

Toasted Sesame Seed Vinaigrette

MAKES ABOUT 1 ½ CUPS

1 T. Sesame seeds
2 tsp. Ginger-minced
1 tsp. Garlic-minced
2 T. Honey
1 T. Soy sauce
* 2 tsp. Sriracha-asian hot sauce
½ C. Rice wine vinegar
¾ C. Grapeseed oil
¼ C. Sesame oil
1 T. Fresh Cilantro-chopped
1 T. Green onion-sliced thin

In a dry, hot skillet add sesame seeds and toast for about 1 minute, stirring constantly to keep from burning. Remove sesame seeds from pan and place in a mixing bowl. Add ginger, garlic, honey, soy sauce, sriracha and rice wine vinegar. Stir together. Slowly whisk in grapeseed oil, then sesame oil until dressing is emulsified. Stir in cilantro and green onion. Will stay a week in the refrigerator.

Maybe the papaya seeds don't add a great deal to this dressing,
I just hated throwing them out.

Papaya Seed Vinaigrette

MAKES 2 CUPS

1 C. Papaya-diced
1 T. Fresh papaya seeds
1 T. Shallots-minced
2 tsp. Dijon mustard
2 T. Honey
¼ C. Fresh squeezed orange juice
¼ C. Balsamic vinegar
½ C. Grapeseed oil

Place all ingredients, except oil, in a blender. Blend on high until smooth. With blender running slowly pour in grapeseed oil to emulsify. Serve with your favorite salad.

Fresh Orange Thyme Vinaigrette

MAKES ABOUT 1 ½ CUPS

3 Navel oranges-peeled, pith removed, rough chopped
1 T. Red onion-minced
1 T. Fresh squeezed lime juice
¼ C. Honey
1 T. Dijon mustard
¼ C. Rice wine vinegar
¼ C. Grapeseed oil
1 T. Fresh thyme leaves
Salt & pepper to taste

In a blender add oranges, red onion, lime juice, honey, mustard and vinegar. Blend on high until mixture is completely smooth. With blender on high slowly add grapeseed oil until dressing thickens. Season with salt, fresh ground black pepper and thyme leaves. Great with grilled lobster or fish.

* Omit the oil in this dressing and you have a wonderful fat free vinaigrette great to toss on baby greens or your favorite salad.

This recipe is mentioned with the Warm Skate Salad. However, the flavors of this vinaigrette bode well for many a dish.

Toasted Coriander Seed-Orange Vinaigrette

MAKES ABOUT 1 CUP

1 T. Cracked coriander seeds
2 tsp. Shallots
2 T. Dry sherry
2 T. Rice wine vinegar
1 T. Balsamic vinegar
½ C. Fresh squeezed orange juice
⅓ C. olive oil
1 T. Fresh basil-chopped
Salt and fresh ground pepper to taste

Heat a medium sauté pan until very hot. Add coriander seeds and stir for 1 minute. Add shallots, sherry, rice and balsamic vinegar. Cook for 1 minute. Add orange juice and heat until warm. Whisk in olive oil, and remove from heat. Season with salt and pepper. Stir in basil. Serve vinaigrette warm.

Caramelized Red Onion Marmalade

4 C. Red onion-diced
2 T. Butter
1 C. Red wine vinegar
¼ C. Port
¼ C. Sugar
1 T. Fresh thyme leaves or 1 tsp. dry thyme

Heat butter in large sauté pan over high heat. Add onions and cook for 3 minutes, stirring occasionally. Add wine vinegar, port, sugar and lower heat to medium. Reduce mixture until liquid has evaporated and given the onions a beautiful glaze. Stir in thyme and salt and pepper to taste. This may be prepared ahead and kept in the refrigerator for up to a week.

* Wonderful on grilled steaks, swordfish or even a roast turkey sandwich.

Pickled Onions

. . . .

2 C. Onions-diced
1 ½ C. Red wine vinegar
3 T. Sugar
1 T. Ginger-minced
1 tsp. Cumin seeds-crushed
1 tsp. Coriander seeds-crushed

In a heavy-bottomed saucepan bring vinegar, sugar, ginger, cumin and corian-der to a simmer. Add onions and cook slowly for about 10 minutes. Remove from heat and let cool. Strain onions from remaining liquid. Refrigerate onions for up to 2 weeks. Great on sandwiches, grilled chicken or steak.

For the ancho chiles, you can substitute roasted peppers or eggplant, caramel-ized onions, cooked shrimp or lobster. Any fresh herb can be substituted for the cilantro. The variations for this recipe are endless.

Ancho Chile Butter

. . . .

1 Lb. Unsalted butter
2 Large ancho chiles-dried
1 T. Cilantro-chopped (optional)

Bring butter to room temperature in bowl of mixer. Place chiles in a large bowl and cover with boiling water. When peppers have rehydrated, drain well. Remove stems and seeds and place in a food processor and puree until smooth.

Whip butter on high in mixing bowl until smooth. Add peppers and cilantro and mix until thoroughly combined. Use as a topping for grilled fish, chicken or steaks. Can be refrigerated or frozen for later use.

Clarified Butter

. . . .

Place butter in a saucepan and melt over low heat. This will allow the milk solids to fall to the bottom of the pan. When completely melted, remove from heat and let sit for 5 minutes. Carefully pour off the clear yellow butter and discard the white sediment on the bottom. The clarified butter is very good for sautéed dishes as it has a higher heating point. Will keep 2 months in your refrigerator. This recipe will be referred to throughout the book.

You can do this on your outdoor grill also. I do these at home in the late summer months. You can go to a local farm stand and get a bushel of peppers for less than 10 dollars at times. Make a whole bunch and freeze in small amounts.

Roasted Red Peppers

6 Large red peppers
Olive oil for brushing peppers

Brush peppers with olive oil. Place peppers on a broiler pan and place under a preheated broiler 2 inches from heat source. Turn peppers every 5 minutes or so for about 15 minutes. You want skins to be blistered and charred. Place peppers in a bowl and cover tightly with aluminum foil. When peppers have cooled, remove skin- it should peel easily. Remove core and seeds. I like to toss the peppers with fresh chopped garlic and olive oil. Keep refrigerated. Refer to this recipe whenever roasted peppers are called for.

Homemade Mayonnaise

MAKES ABOUT 2 CUPS

4 egg Yolks
1 Egg
1 tsp. Dijon mustard
3 tsp. Red wine vinegar
2 tsp. Fresh lemon juice
1 ½ C. Grapeseed or olive oil
Salt and white pepper to taste

In a food processor mix egg yolks, egg and mustard until thick. With processor on drizzle in vinegar, lemon juice and then oil. Blend thoroughly. Season with salt and pepper. Refrigerate immediately.

Salads

Salad Greens

· · · · · · · · · · · · · · · · · · · ·

We are all familiar with the basics found in stores today-iceberg, romaine, green and red leaf and bibb lettuce. However, there is a much larger variety of less used lettuces in stores today that include arugula, radicchio, oak leaf, frisee and mesclun.

Mesclun is becoming one of the most popular in today's supermarket. Mesclun can be a mix of just about any number of greens-arugula, mache, mizuna, frisee, radicchio, sorrel, dandelion and oak leaf to name a few. Mesclun mix gives you a beautiful array of shapes, colors and flavors. It is most often sold in bulk by the pound, but has recently become available prepacked. Mesclun is very fragile. Be sure leaves are firm and crisp with no signs of wilting or moisture. You can refrigerate in a plastic bag anywhere from 3-5 days. When I mention mixed baby greens throughout the book I am referring to mesclun mix.

The following chapter holds a varied assortment of salads. The term "salad" today has a much broader definition. They can range from first courses, such as the Strawberry Gorgonzola Salad to accompaniments, such as the Marinated Fennel Salad to main courses-Pan Roasted Skate Wing Salad. However, many of the following recipes can be modified to serve as a starter or an entrée.

Grilled Key West Shrimp with Crab Chutney and Caramelized Papaya-Mango Vinaigrette

SERVES 6

30 Fresh Key West shrimp U-15 (peeled and deveined)
4 T. Olive oil
Salt and pepper to taste
1 Lb. Jumbo lump crab
1 C. Ripe papaya (cut into a fine dice)
1 C. Ripe mango (cut into a fine dice)
1 tsp. Snipped chives
1 T. Red bell pepper (finely diced)
20 C. Assorted baby greens
1 ½ C. Caramelized papaya mango vinaigrette (recipe below)

Toss shrimp with olive oil, salt and pepper. Grill shrimp over high heat for 1 ½ minutes on each side. Remove and keep warm. Lightly toss crab, papaya, mango, chives and red bell pepper. Keep chilled. Toss greens with 1 cup of vinaigrette. Place remaining vinaigrette in squirt bottle for garnish. Place 2 cups of greens in center of plate. Place 3 shrimp on edge of greens and top each shrimp with 1 ounce of crab chutney. Garnish perimeter of each plate with remaining dressing. A nice garnish is crispy fried julienne leeks or crispy fried yams.

Caramelized Papaya-Mango Vinaigrette

3 C. Red wine vinegar
1 ½ C. Sugar
1 T. Poblano pepper (minced)
1 Ripe papaya (seeded and chopped)
1 Ripe mango (seeded and chopped)
¼ C. Passion fruit juice concentrate
⅓ C. Guava puree
⅓ C. Pineapple juice

In heavy bottomed saucepan over medium high heat, combine red wine vinegar, sugar and Poblano pepper. Bring to boil, then lower heat to a simmer. Reduce mixture for 5 minutes. Add papaya and mango, and reduce mixture until lightly caramelized. Place caramel mixture in blender and emulsify. Add passion fruit juice, guava puree and pineapple juice. Blend until smooth. Season with salt and pepper. Keep at room temperature. Serve with grilled Key West shrimp salad.

Serving suggestion: This is a fat free dressing that goes well with chicken, fish, shellfish or just with mixed greens.

Grilled Jumbo Shrimp with Mediterranean Cous Cous Salad

. . . .

SERVES 6

1 T. Olive oil	1 C. Feta Cheese
½ C. Onion-diced	1 C. Calamata olives-pitted & halved
2 T. Garlic-minced	2 T. Capers
2 ½ C. Chicken stock	2 T. Basil-chopped
12 oz. Cous Cous	Salt & pepper to taste
6 C. Arugula-rinsed & dried	2 C. Canned plum tomatoes-diced
¼ C. Extra virgin olive oil	24 Jumbo shrimp-peeled & deveined
¼ C. Balsamic vinegar	3 T. Olive oil

Place a medium saucepan over medium high heat. Add olive oil, onion and garlic and sauté for 2-3 minutes. Add chicken stock and bring to a boil. Stir in cous cous, remove from heat and cover. Let stand until chicken stock is absorbed, about 5 minutes. Fluff cous cous with a fork and place in a large mixing bowl. Add plum tomatoes, extra virgin olive oil and balsamic vinegar and toss together. Let cous cous cool, stirring occasionally to release heat. When cool add feta cheese, olives, capers, basil and salt and pepper. Refrigerate until chilled.

Remove cous cous from refrigerator 20 minutes before serving. Toss shrimp with olive oil and season with salt and pepper. Grill over medium high heat for 2-3 minutes per side.

For service-divide cous cous evenly among 6 plates. Sprinkle each plate with arugula. Garnish with 4 jumbo shrimp. Serve with balsamic or roasted garlic vinaigrette on the side.

Here are two easy salads that can be served anytime of the year. You can substitute shrimp or crabmeat in the Asian Lobster Salad.

Jumbo Lump Crab Salad with Avocado Mayonnaise

1 Lb. Jumbo lump crabmeat-shells removed
¼ C. Diced red pepper
¼ C. Diced yellow pepper
¼ C. Diced red onion
2 T. Cilantro-chopped
1 T. Chives-snipped
½ C. Mayonnaise
¾ C. Avocado-diced
1 T. Fresh lemon juice
1 tsp. Tabasco sauce
Salt to taste

Mix jumbo lump crab, red and yellow pepper, red onion, cilantro and chives. In a separate bowl gently toss mayonnaise, avocado, lemon juice, tabasco and salt to taste. Toss crab mixture with avocado mayonnaise. Serve crab salad on a bed of your favorite mixed greens and sliced tomato.

Asian Lobster Salad

SERVES 4-6

1 ½ Lbs. Cooked lobster meat
1 C. Snow peas-blanched & julienned
½ C. Red pepper-julienned
½ C. Yellow pepper-julienned
½ C. Carrots-julienned
½ C. Bean sprouts
Toasted sesame seed vinaigrette (see recipe in dressing chapter)

Cut lobster into bite size pieces. Toss with vegetables. Can be made up to 4 hours ahead to this point. When ready to serve toss with toasted sesame seed vinaigrette and serve on bed of mixed greens.

This may be my favorite recipe in the book. Skate is a flavorful, underutilized fish, that is complemented quite well by the coriander seed dressing. You can substitute your favorite greens for the micro greens listed here (we get the micro greens from local farmers).

Pan Roasted Skate Wing Salad, Micro Greens and Heirloom Tomatoes

2 T. Clarified butter
1 Lb. Boneless skate wing (about 4 oz each)
Flour seasoned with salt & pepper
1 T. Cracked coriander seeds
2 tsp. Shallots, minced
2 T. Dry sherry
2 T. Rice wine vinegar
1 T. Balsamic vinegar
½ C. Fresh squeezed orange juice
⅓ C. Olive oil
1 T. Fresh basil, chopped
6 C. Assorted micro greens (baby bulls blood, arugula, amaranth, chrysanthemum, tatsoi)
1 C. Heirloom tomatoes, diced
1 C. Skinless orange segments, diced
2 T. Capers

Heat a large sauté pan and add clarified butter. Dredge skate fillets in seasoned flour. Add skate to pan and cook for 2-3 minutes per side. They should have a nice golden color. Remove from pan and keep warm.

Add coriander seeds to sauté pan and cook for 1 minute, stirring constantly. Add shallots and deglaze pan with sherry, rice wine and balsamic vinegar. Reduce mixture for 1 minute. Add orange juice and heat through. Whisk in olive oil and remove from heat. Season with salt and pepper. Stir in basil.

Place 1 ½ cup greens in center of each plate. Cut skate fillets into strips, following division in fish. Place skate atop greens. Drizzle skate and greens with coriander seed vinaigrette. Sprinkle perimeter of plate with heirloom tomatoes, orange segments and capers.

Grilled Vegetable Salad

1 Small eggplant, peeled & cut into ½ in. thick rounds
1 Medium zucchini, sliced diagonally ½ in. thick
1 Medium yellow squash, sliced diagonally ½ in. thick
1 medium red onion, peeled and cut into ½ in. thick rounds
Olive oil for brushing vegetables
Salt and fresh ground pepper
1 C. Roasted peppers (see recipe)
8 Slices beefsteak tomatoes
8 Slices fresh mozzarella
8 C. Mixed baby greens
Roasted garlic vinaigrette (see recipe in dressing chapter)

Brush eggplant, zucchini, squash and red onion with olive oil on both sides. Season with salt and pepper. Place vegetables on a hot grill and cook for 2 minutes on each side.

Place 2 cups greens on a large plate. Fan eggplant, zucchini and squash on one side of greens. Fan alternate slices of 2 tomato and 2 mozzarella on other side. Top each salad with grilled red onions and roasted peppers. Garnish with roasted garlic vinaigrette.

Cucumber and Feta Cheese Salad

MAKES ABOUT 4 CUPS

1 ½ C. Cucumbers, peeled, seeded and sliced
1 C. Crumbled feta cheese
½ C. Roasted red peppers, chopped
½ C. Calamata olives, pitted and chopped
½ C. Red onion, thin julienne
2 T. Fresh basil, chopped
¼ C. Balsamic vinegar
⅓ C. Extra virgin olive oil
Fresh ground black pepper

Toss cucumbers, feta cheese, roasted peppers, olives, red onions and basil in a mixing bowl. Add vinegar, oil and fresh ground black pepper. Toss together and let sit at least 1 hour. Serve salad tossed with mixed greens, as a side dish to grilled chicken or as an appetizer over grilled French bread.

Here is a perfect accompaniment to your favorite grilled steak. You could also add grilled shrimp or chicken and serve it as a light main course.

Warm Wild Mushroom Salad

SERVES 4

3 T. Unsalted butter
1 T. Shallots-minced
4 C. wild mushrooms-sliced (including portabello, shiitake, crimini or oyster)
3 T. Dry sherry
1 T. Worcestershire sauce
1 T. Fresh thyme leaves
Salt & fresh ground pepper to taste
⅓ C. Balsamic vinegar
1 T. Dijon mustard
½ C. Olive oil
8 C. Mixed baby greens
2 T. Capers
8 oz. Chevre, crumbled

In a large sauté pan melt butter over high heat. Add shallots and mushrooms and cook for 5-7 minutes, stirring occasionally, until mushrooms are softened. Add sherry and worcestershire sauce and cook additional 2 minutes. Add thyme and season with salt and pepper. Keep warm.

In a mixing bowl combine balsamic vinegar and dijon mustard. Slowly whisk in olive oil in a steady stream until emulsified. Toss baby greens with dressing. Place 2 cups greens on each plate. Sprinkle with warm mushrooms. Garnish with capers and crumbled chevre. Serve immediately.

Strawberries and gorgonzola were meant for each other unless you're serving figs. This light summer salad is always a hit. You can substitute toasted almonds for the honey caramelized pecans.

Strawberry-Gorgonzola Salad

SERVE 4

8 C. Assorted baby greens
1 C. Gorgonzola-crumbled
1 C. Red grapes
1 C. Honey caramelized pecans (see recipe)
1 C. Fresh strawberries-halved
2 T. Honey
2 tsp. Dijon mustard
¼ C. Balsamic vinegar
¼ C. Olive oil
Salt & pepper to taste

In a large bowl lightly toss greens, gorgonzola, grapes, pecans and strawberries. In a separate bowl mix honey, dijon mustard and balsamic vinegar. Slowly whisk in olive oil to emulsify dressing. Season with salt and pepper. Pour dressing over salad, toss lightly and serve.

Balsamic Glazed Figs and Gorgonzola

12 Black mission figs
2 T. Honey-warmed
½ C. Balsamic vinegar
½ Lb. Gorgonzola
Multigrain or dense walnut bread

Preheat oven to 375°. Slice figs in half and brush cut sides with warmed honey. Place figs on a baking sheet, cut side facing up. Bake until figs are warmed through-about 10 minutes. Remove from oven and keep warm.

In a small saucepan place balsamic vinegar over high heat and reduce by half until lightly syrupy.

Place figs on serving platter and top with crumbled gorgonzola cheese. Drizzle with reduced balsamic vinegar. Serve with warmed bread.

Here is a nice alternative to regular potato salad. Try it at your next barbecue. And, yes, I do like gorgonzola!

Potato and Vegetable Salad with Gorgonzola

3 Lb. Small new potatoes
2 tsp. Garlic-minced
2 tsp. Shallots-minced
1 T. Fresh thyme-minced
¼ C. Red wine vinegar
2 T. Dijon mustard
½ C. Olive oil
½ C. Red onion-diced
½ C. Celery-diced
½ C. Carrots-diced

¼ C. Red pepper-diced
¼ C. Yellow pepper-diced
3 Hard boiled eggs-chopped
2 T. Parsley-chopped
2 T. Fresh tarragon-chopped
2 T. Capers
½ C. Mayonnaise
½ C. Gorgonzola-crumbled

Cook potatoes in boiling water until tender, about 25 minutes.

Drain and place in a single layer to cool. Cut potatoes in quarters and set aside.

In a large mixing bowl combine garlic, shallots, thyme, vinegar and dijon mustard. Whisk in olive oil slowly to emulsify dressing. Add potatoes and gently toss to coat potatoes. Refrigerate 2-8 hours.

Remove potatoes from refrigerator. Add onion, celery, carrots, peppers, eggs, parsley, tarragon & capers. Toss lightly to combine vegetables but not break potatoes.

Combine mayonnaise and gorgonzola and gently fold into potato salad. Mix well and serve.

I can't take credit for this one.
This is compliments of my wife, Lenore.

Tomato, Green Bean and Mint Salad

4 C. Ripe tomatoes-cored and cut into small wedges
4 C. Fresh green beans-blanched & cooled in ice bath
1 C. Red onion-julienned
⅓ C. Extra virgin olive oil
¼ C. Balsamic vinegar
½ tsp. Salt
3 T. Fresh mint-chopped
1 T. Basil-chopped
Fresh ground black pepper

In a large mixing bowl toss tomatoes, green beans, red onion, olive oil, vinegar and salt. Let marinate up to 6 hours in refrigerator. Add fresh mint, basil and fresh ground black pepper. Let sit 30 minutes at room temperature and serve.

Marinated Fennel Salad

2 Fennel bulbs
2 C. Artichoke hearts-quartered
1 C. Tomatoes-diced
¼ C. Red onion-thin julienne
¼ C. Calamata olives-pitted & halved
¼ C. Olive oil
2 T. Balsamic vinegar
1 t. Fresh lemon juice
2 tsp. Garlic-minced
2 tsp. Fresh oregano or ¼ tsp. dried
2 tsp. Fresh thyme or ¼ tsp. dried
Salt and pepper to taste
2 C. Arugula leaves-rinsed & dried (optional)

Trim top of fennel where stalks meet the bulb and discard (or save for stock). Cut bulbs in half and remove core from each. Slice fennel very thin. In a large bowl toss fennel, artichoke hearts, tomatoes, onion, olives, olive oil, vinegar, lemon juice, garlic, oregano & thyme. Mix thoroughly and refrigerate up to 8 hours. Season with salt and pepper. Toss with arugula leaves just before serving.

Marinated Mushroom Salad

· · · · · · · · · · · · · · · · · · · ·

2 C. Medium mushrooms-cut in half
1 C. Cucumbers-halved, seeded and sliced
½ C. Red onion-julienned
1 T. Garlic-minced
2 T. Honey
2 T. Fresh basil-chopped
½ C. Balsamic vinegar
½ C. Diced tomatoes in puree
2 tsp. Dried thyme
½ C. Olive oil
Salt & pepper to taste

In a large bowl combine mushrooms, cucumbers and red onion. In a separate bowl combine garlic, honey, basil, balsamic vinegar, diced tomatoes and thyme. Slowly whisk in olive oil. Season with salt and fresh ground black pepper. Toss mushroom salad with balsamic marinade. Let sit at least 3 hours. Serve as a salad or tossed with mixed greens. Will keep in refrigerator for 2 days.

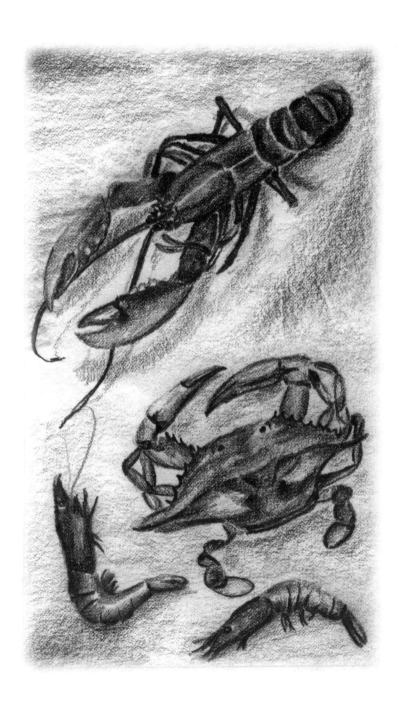

Seafood

Shellfish

As with fish, the versatility of shellfish is endless. At Radnor we have the fortune of fresh spiny lobsters, Key West shrimp and stone crab claws from Florida. Beautiful firm sweet diver scallops and Atlantic lobsters from Maine and softshell crabs from Maryland. The following is a few tips in finding the best your local markets have to offer.

Lobsters

When purchasing lobsters, be sure they are alive-it should curl its tail and flay its claws when picked up. If not cooked right after purchasing, it is best kept in the crisper drawer of your refrigerator. Cover lobster with damp newspaper to keep alive. When purchasing cooked lobsters, be sure tail is curled under. This shows lobster was alive when cooked.

A side note to purchasing North Atlantic lobsters in the late summer months-they grow new shells-these soft shell lobsters yield less meat and have inferior flavor and texture.

Soft Shell Crabs

When buying soft shells they must be alive. If you are going to prepare them right away, you can ask your fish market to clean them. If not, you will need to clean them yourself. Trim the eyes, lift the top flaps and remove the featherlike gills. Then, cut away the tail from the bottom apron. Gently squeeze to remove the green bubble from the center (this is somewhat bitter). You can always ask for a quick tip when purchasing.

Sea Scallops

I prefer to use only dry sea scallops. A large majority of sea scallops are soaked in a phosphate solution on the fishing boats. This preservative makes the scallops plump, but when cooked the liquid is released and your sautéed sea scallops become steamed. Ask your fish market for the possibility of getting dry sea scallops. I also use diver scallops whenever possible. These are hand harvested scallops that are delivered live in the shell. Divers are much meatier and firm than regular sea scallops. They are difficult to get, but worth the expense.

Stone Crab Claws

Primarily fished off the coast of Florida. These crabs have large, meaty claws, but are otherwise inedible. They will always be sold cooked. When stone crabs are caught the crabber removes one claw and throws it back in the water. The crab will eventually grow back the claw. This process helps perpetuate the species, but also makes it an expensive delicacy.

Shrimp

There are over 300 species worldwide but only a few important to the United States. There are three basic groups-warmwater, coldwater and freshwater. They are both farm raised and wild-caught.

Warmwater – The most plentiful and popular shrimp in the United States. They are grouped into categories by the color of their shell when raw-white, brown, black tiger and pink. The flavor of these shrimp vary depending on where they are caught or raised and what their diet consists of. White and brown are the most used type in the United States. However, tiger shrimp (named for the black stripes on their shells when raw) are becoming a big hit in the aqua culture industry. Raised primarily in Asian countries, these shrimp have a higher moisture content, resulting in a milder flavor. I think the flavor is inferior to the others. Overall, I prefer brown shrimp from the Gulf Coast, which live in kelp rich waters. The iodine rich diet gives the shrimp a wonderful flavor. Pink shrimp are caught in the same waters as the brown and white and give you a shrimp with a firm texture and sweet flavor.

Coldwater – These shrimp are caught off the coasts of Oregon, Washington and Alaska, as well as from the coasts of Iceland and Norway. They are referred to as bay shrimp or baby shrimp. They are very small compared to their warmwater counterparts and are generally sold peeled and cooked. They range anywhere from 150-400 shrimp per pound.

Freshwater – These shrimp are generally characterized by a bright, blue shell. They have long claws and may weigh up to one pound and grow a foot long. These shrimp have a rather mild flavor and consist of a very small portion of the market. You will sometimes see them presented live in restaurant display tanks.

Purchasing Shrimp

You will find that shrimp are sold by size. The smaller the number, the larger the shrimp. For example, a shrimp labeled U-15 means that there are under 15 shrimp to a pound. A shrimp labeled 26-30 means there are between 26 and 30 shrimp per pound. You may also see shrimp labeled 60/ov which means there are over 60 to the pound. Some places may sell shrimp as small, medium and large, however, they should also be accompanied by a number. If not, ask!! So remember, the smaller the number, the larger the shrimp-and higher the price.

You can purchase shrimp in supermarkets in a 5 lb. block. If you only want a portion of that, run the shrimp under **cold** water until you have thawed the amount you need. Wrap the remaining shrimp and place in a plastic bag and put in your freezer. A frozen block in its original package can last up to 16 months at a temperature of 0°or less. In the freezer of your basic home refrigerator a time span of 3-4 months.

Be aware that shrimp you buy from your local markets seafood case is not "fresh shrimp." They have already been thawed out, so it is a good idea to not refreeze. Check for a healthy appearance and almost no smell. If you detect a hint of ammonia, the product is on its way out. Do not be afraid to check!

The Perfect Shrimp Cocktail

Fill a large pot with water ⅔ full. Add your favorite seasonings, such as Old Bay, bay leaf, red pepper flakes, fresh lemon and coriander seed. Bring to a boil and add thawed shrimp. * Do not remove the shells until after cooking. Cook uncovered 3-4 ½ minutes for sizes 16/20 and larger, 2-3 minutes for sizes 21/25-31/35. The shrimp should be firm and white throughout. You can always cut one open to be sure. Remove shrimp from pot and immediately place in a bath of ice water to stop the cooking process. Peel shell, remove black vein from back of shrimp and serve.

Peekytoe Crabs

I am only mentioning peekytoe crabs because I find it such an interesting story. The peekytoe crab has been, for many years, the throwaway byproduct of Maine lobstermen. However, with the aid of some of the countries most influential chefs a pound of peekytoe crabmeat can sell for as much as $14 per pound.

For years Maine crabmeat has been sold and has contained the meat of Maine Red, Jonah or Peekytoe crabs, or a combination of the three. Unfortunately, there are many seafood wholesalers who sell peekytoe but are not always true in keeping it separate from the other crabmeat. It is for this reason that a chef must know his source in Maine to be assured that he is receiving the real thing.

This crab, known as a rock crab, sand crab or mudcrab, has a very delicate, sweet flavor that lends itself to simple preparations. In Maine it is simply mixed with mayonnaise and stuffed in a toasted, buttered bun, much like the famous Maine lobster roll.

The peekytoe crab industry was actually started by the wives of Maine lobsterman. They persuaded their husbands to keep the crabs in the slower months so that they could make some extra money. They cooked and picked the crabs in their house and sold their crabmeat to a seafood wholesaler in Portland, Maine.

The wholesaler, in turn, convinced a handful of top chefs in New York City of the unique flavor of the peekytoe. Soon, as with any new industry, the government stepped in with stricter guidelines on processing the crabs, putting many small pickers out of business. The crabs now have to be cooked and cleaned in a structure separate from their houses.

Unfortunately, you cannot go into a local market and buy true Peekytoe crabmeat. However, if you find yourself driving along the coast in Maine, look for signs on resident mailboxes reading "Crabmeat for sale." You may just have happened upon one of the wives who began this new business.

This is an easy preparation that makes an outdoor BBQ with friends extra special. To save some time, you can cook the lobsters up to a day ahead of time. However, don't split the lobsters until you are ready to grill (this will prevent them from losing moisture).

Grilled New England Lobster with Mustard Sauce

½ Lb. Softened butter
¼ C. Dijon mustard
¼ C. Coarse mustard
1 T. Garlic-minced
1 T. Shallots-minced
2 T. Fresh basil-chopped
1 T. Fresh snipped chives
4-1 ¾ lb. live lobsters
2 T. Salt

In a mixing bowl combine softened butter, mustards, garlic, shallots, basil and chives. Mix thoroughly.

Fill a large stockpot with water. Add salt and bring water to a boil. Add lobsters and cook for 8 minutes. Remove lobsters from pot.

Split lobsters down the middle in half. Brush cut tail section with mustard mixture. Place lobsters over a medium hot grill, split side up and grill for 5 minutes. Turn lobsters and grill an additional 2-3 minutes. This may also be accomplished under a broiler if a grill is not available.

Lobster and Corn Custard with Smoked Yellow Pepper Oil and Roasted Red Pepper Puree

SERVES 4

1 C. White corn kernels (cut from 2 ears corn)
2 Eggs
2 Egg yolks
½ C. Heavy cream
2 tsp. Dijon mustard
2 tsp. Old Bay
1 tsp. Tabasco
1 T. Basil-chopped
8 oz. Cooked lobster meat, diced
½ C. Roasted red peppers (pureed in a food processor until smooth)

In a food processor blend half of corn with eggs, yolks, heavy cream, dijon mustard, Old Bay and tabasco until smooth. Stir in basil and remaining corn.

Preheat oven to 350°. Butter 4-six ounce ramekins. Place 2 ounces lobster in each cup. Pour custard into cups. Set in a baking pan and fill with hot water until ramekins are covered halfway. Cover pan and bake in center of oven for 20-25 minutes. Remove foil and cook additional 5 minutes to brown lightly.

Remove ramekins from water and let sit 2-3 minutes. Carefully remove custards from cups and serve browned side up. Garnish each plate with smoked yellow pepper oil, roasted red pepper puree and fresh snipped chives.

Smoked Yellow Pepper Oil

· ·

2 Large yellow peppers
½ C. Mesquite wood chips, soaked for 15 minutes
¼ C. Olive oil
Juicer

Place wood chips in bottom of stovetop smoker. Place grate in smoker and set peppers on top. Cover and place over medium heat. When chips begin to smoke reduce heat to low. Smoke for 10 minutes. Remove from heat and let stand 30 minutes.

Remove peppers from smoker. Core and seed peppers. Place yellow peppers in a juicer. You will get anywhere from 3-5 ounces of pepper juice.

Place pepper juice in a blender. With machine on high slowly pour in olive oil to emulsify. Place in a squirt bottle to garnish.

Grilled Lobster Tails with Orange Thyme Vinaigrette

· ·

SERVES 6

12 -4 oz. Cold water lobster tails (removed from shells)
¼ C. Olive oil
1 T. Shallots
2 T. Fresh chopped basil

Score bottom of lobster tails with a sharp knife. Three small slits will be enough. This will keep the lobster from curling during cooking. Toss lobster tails with olive oil, shallots and basil. Let marinate up to 4 hours. Grill lobster tails for 3 minutes on each side, or until cooked through. You can serve the lobster tails on a bed of mixed baby greens and sliced Heirloom tomatoes or grilled vegetables. Drizzle with orange thyme vinaigrette (see recipe in Dressings Chapter).

My two sons, Joshua and Dylan, love this dish. I can't make enough when it comes to fried calamari. Unless, of course, I'm serving them steamed mussels or clams.

Crispy Calamari with Spicy Sweet Dipping Sauce

¾ C. Rice wine vinegar
3 T. Sugar
1 tsp. Salt
* 2 T. Sriracha (asian hot sauce)
2 tsp. Ginger-minced
1 tsp. Garlic-minced
1 T. Scallions-chopped thin
1 T. Fresh cilantro-chopped
2 Lb. Small squid-totally cleaned, tubes cut into ½ inch thick rings
2 C. Flour
2 tsp. Salt and ¼ tsp. Black pepper
1 tsp. Paprika
* *Available in Chinese markets*

In a small saucepan add vinegar, sugar, salt and sriracha. Cook over medium heat for about 10 minutes or until sugar has dissolved. Remove from heat and stir in ginger and garlic. Let cool, then add scallions and cilantro.

Mix flour, salt, pepper and paprika in a large bowl. Toss squid, a little at a time, in seasoned flour. Fry squid in batches in a 375° fryer for 2-3 minutes. Drain on paper towels, serve with spicy-sweet dipping sauce.

The tequila gives this dish a very unique flavor. Along with the honey, it will give the shrimp a sweet, caramelized glaze when grilled. Enough for a dinner or when made in a smaller portion-a great first course.

Tequila Lime Grilled Shrimp with Avocado and Proscuitto

SERVES 4

1 C. Gold Tequila
¼ C. Fresh lime juice
1 T. Garlic-minced
1 T. Ginger-minced
2 T. Honey
1 T. Grapeseed oil
2 tsp. Ground cumin seed
2 tsp. Ground coriander seed
20 Jumbo shrimp (U-15) peeled & deveined
2 Avocado-cored, peeled & sliced
1 pt. Teardrop tomatoes
8 Thin slices proscuitto-baked in 400° oven for 6 minutes or until crispy, then crumbled
8 C. Assorted baby greens
Papaya Seed Vinaigrette (see recipe in Dressing Chapter)

In a small saucepan place tequila and cook over high heat until reduced by half. Remove from heat. Stir in garlic, ginger, honey, grapeseed oil, cumin and coriander. Place shrimp in a mixing bowl and toss with cooled tequila marinade. Let sit 1-2 hours. Carefully spray a hot grill with non-stick cooking spray. Grill shrimp for 2-3 minutes on each side until cooked through. Remove from grill and keep warm.

Toss greens with 1 cup papaya seed vinaigrette. Place 2 cups greens on each plate. Garnish with half of a sliced avocado, teardrop tomatoes and 5 shrimp. Sprinkle with crispy proscuitto.

This recipe is great for anytime of the year. It can be served as an hors d'oeuvres, first course or entrée. Just a reminder, be sure to remove the zest from the citrus before cutting and squeezing juice.

Ginger and Citrus Roasted Shrimp

SERVES 4

20 Jumbo shrimp-peeled and butterflied
½ C. Fresh squeezed orange juice
¼ C. Fresh squeezed lemon juice
¼ C. Fresh squeezed lime juice
¼ C. Brown sugar
2 T. Orange zest-minced
1 T. Lemon zest-minced
1 T. Lime zest-minced
2 t. Kosher salt
2 T. Pickled ginger-minced
2 T. & 2 T. Olive oil
4 T. Grande Marnier

In a small saucepan combine citrus juice and brown sugar. Bring mixture to a simmer and reduce to about a ¼ cup. Stir in citrus zests, salt and pickled ginger. Simmer an additional 2 minutes and remove from heat and let cool.

Toss shrimp with citrus reduction pressing mixture into shrimp. Place a large sauté pan over high heat. Add 2 T. olive oil to pan and sear half of the shrimp for 1 minute on each side. Remove from pan and add additional 2 T. oil if needed. Sear other half of shrimp for same amount of time. Add first batch of shrimp to pan and carefully pour in Grande Marnier. Toss shrimp in pan for 1-2 minutes and serve.

Tired of clams in white or red sauce? Try this recipe next time.
You can make it a meal by serving over your favorite pasta.

Steamed Littleneck Clams with Ancho Chile Pesto Broth

. . . .

SERVES 4

48 Littleneck clams
8 Ancho chiles-dried
4 New Mexico red chiles-dried
8 Cloves garlic
⅓ C. Pine nuts-toasted
1 T. Fresh basil
1 T. Parsley
⅓ C. Olive oil
3 T. Fresh lemon juice
4 C. Clam juice
½ C. Dry white wine
3 T. Cilantro-chopped

Roast chiles in a preheated 400° oven for 3-4 minutes. Remove stems and seeds. Place chiles in a bowl. Pour boiling water on chiles and let sit until very soft, about 30 minutes.

In a food processor combine chiles, garlic, pine nuts, basil and parsley. You may need to add some of the olive oil to help process the mixture. Puree until smooth. With the processor on slowly pour in remaining olive oil and lemon juice.

Meanwhile, rinse clams and discard any opened ones. In a large saucepan, heat clam juice and white wine. Bring to a boil. Add clams, reduce to a simmer and cover. When clams begin to open remove from pan and keep warm. Reduce clam juice by about half and then whisk in ancho chile pesto.

Place clams in soup bowls and ladle pesto mixture over them. Sprinkle with chopped cilantro.

Steamed Mussels with Fresh Herb Mustard Sauce
. . . .

2 Lb. Mussels (washed in cold water, beards removed)
1 T. Olive oil
1 C. Onion-minced
2 T. Fresh garlic-minced
½ tsp. Red pepper flakes
½ C. Dry white wine

In a large stockpot heat olive oil. Sauté onions and garlic for about 2 minutes. Add white wine, red pepper flakes and mussels and cover pot. Steam mussels for 4-5 minutes or until mussels are opened. Remove mussels to a serving platter, discarding any unopened shells. Drizzle mussels with the remaining wine mixture from stockpot. Serve with fresh herb mustard sauce.

Fresh Herb Mustard Sauce
. . . .

MAKES ABOUT 1 CUP

3 T. Dijon mustard
1 T. Balsamic vinegar
1 T. Fresh lemon juice
½ C. Olive oil
2 tsp. Shallots-minced
1 T. Fresh dill-chopped
1 T. Fresh tarragon-chopped
1 T. Fresh snipped chives
1 T. Capers-minced
Salt and pepper to taste

In a blender, puree dijon mustard, balsamic vinegar and lemon juice. With blender on, slowly add olive oil in a thin stream until emulsified. Remove from processor and stir in shallots, dill, tarragon, chives and capers. Season with salt & pepper. Serve at room temperature.

Crispy Soft Shell Crabs with Grilled Corn & Tomato Salsa

. . . .

Grilled Corn Salsa

. . . .

ABOUT 3 CUPS

3 Ears corn
½ C. Diced tomatoes (peeled & seeded)
¼ C. Roasted red peppers-chopped
½ C. Roasted green chiles-chopped
2 T. Red onion-minced
1 tsp. Garlic-minced
1 T. Cilantro-chopped
1 T. Lime juice
2 T. Extra virgin olive oil

Pull husk of corn back and remove silk. Cover corn back up with husks. Soak corn in cold water for 5-10 minutes. Place corn on medium grill and cook for 4-6 minutes on each side. Let cool and husk corn. Cut kernels from cob, being sure not to cut into the cob itself. Toss corn with tomatoes, peppers, chiles, red onions, garlic, cilantro and lime juice. Stir in olive oil and season with salt.

Soft Shell Crabs

. . . .

8 Jumbo soft shell crabs-gills & aprons removed, eyes trimmed
¾ C. Flour
¾ C. Cornmeal
2 tsp. Ancho chile powder
1 tsp. Salt
1 C. Heavy cream
4 T. Clarified butter

Heat large sauté pan. Add 2 T. Clarified butter. Mix flour, cornmeal, chile powder and salt. Dip crabs in cream, then dredge in flour mixture. Sauté crabs, a few at a time, for 2-3 minutes on each side. Add butter as needed and cook remaining crabs. Top crabs with corn salsa.

You can substitute chicken stock if you don't have any lobster stock available. Be sure to sauté the rice before adding any stock, stirring to keep from sticking. Read about arborio rice in the Pasta & Grains section of this book for added tips on making this tasty dish.

Seafood Risotto

SERVES 6-8

3 C. Lobster or shrimp stock
2 C. Clam juice
3 T. Unsalted butter
1 C. Onion-diced
1 T. Shallots-minced
1 C. Dry white wine
2 C. Canned plum tomatoes-diced
½ C. Parmesan cheese
¼ C. Heavy cream (optional)
2 T. Flat parsley-chopped
2 T. Fresh basil-chopped
Salt & pepper to taste
2 T. Olive oil
1 Lb. Uncooked lobster tail meat, cut into 1 in. pieces
¾ Lb. Raw jumbo shrimp, peeled and deveined
½ Lb. Sea scallops (20-30 Ct)
2 tsp. Garlic-minced

In a medium saucepan heat lobster stock and clam juice. Bring to a simmer and keep warm.

Place a heavy-bottomed saucepan over medium high heat and melt butter. Add onions and shallots and sauté for 3 minutes. Add rice and sauté an additional 2 minutes. Add white wine and cook until liquid is absorbed. Add 1 cup of warm stock to rice, stirring occasionally, until stock is absorbed. Continue adding 1 cup stock in this fashion until all stock is used. Stir in plum tomatoes, parmesan cheese and heavy cream. Keep warm.

Heat 2 T. olive oil in large sauté pan. Add lobster, shrimp, scallops and garlic and sauté for 4-5 minutes until seafood is just cooked through. Add seafood to risotto along with parsley and basil. Season with salt and pepper and serve immediately.

This s a great dish, especially for those of you who don't eat much meat. Portabello mushrooms have a nice meaty texture that is accentuated by grilling. Serves as a first course or omit the crabmeat and serve as a side dish.

Grilled Portabello Mushrooms with Arugula and Crab

. . . .

SERVES 4

1 T. Minced garlic
2 T. Worcestershire
3 T. Balsamic vinegar
2 tsp. Fresh thyme leaves
⅓ C. Olive oil
4 Large Portabello mushrooms
¼ C. White wine
1 T. Shallots-minced
1 C. Plum tomatoes-seeded & chopped
12 oz. Jumbo lump crab (picked)
4 T. Unsalted butter
2 C. Arugula leaves, washed & dried
Salt & pepper to taste

In a large mixing bowl add garlic, worcestershire, balsamic vinegar and thyme. Slowly whisk in olive oil. Pour marinade over mushrooms and let marinate 2 hours.

Grill mushrooms over medium high heat for 2-3 minutes on each side. Remove from grill, cover and keep warm.

In a medium saucepan add white wine and shallots. Cook for about 2 minutes over high heat. Add crabmeat and butter and sauté for additional 2 minutes. Add arugula and cook until it is just wilted. Season with salt and pepper. Serve crab mixture atop grilled portabello mushrooms.

I know there is a bit of heavy cream in this dish but it is worth it. I like to barely cook my scallops through, so you may want to finish your scallops in a 375° oven for about 3 minutes. Don't overcook! You can serve the dish over white rice or your favorite pasta. Voila, dinner is served.

Sautéed Sea Scallops with Dijon Mustard Cream and Jumbo Lump Crab

SERVES 4

20 Jumbo dry sea scallops (U-10)
½ C. Flour
5 T. Grapeseed oil
2 T. Shallots-minced
1 ½ C. Clam juice
1 ½ C. White wine
1 ½ C. Heavy cream
2 T. Coarse mustard
2 T. Dijon mustard
1 T. Fresh chopped tarragon
10 oz. Jumbo lump crabmeat

In a large sauté pan heat grapeseed oil. Dredge scallops in flour. When oil is hot add scallops, a few at a time, cooking for 2 minutes on each side. Remove scallops, season with salt and pepper to taste, and keep warm. Drain oil from pan and deglaze with white wine. Add shallots, clam juice and heavy cream. Reduce mixture by half. Add coarse mustard, dijon mustard, tarragon and jumbo lump crabmeat. Heat through. Serve scallops topped with mustard-crab sauce.

I like to serve these scallops with a mixture of baby arugula, mache and baby frisee. Garnish with crispy fried leeks.

Crispy Leeks: Slice white part of leek, removing root end. Slice in half lengthwise. Julienne leek into thin strips. Wash thoroughly to remove any dirt. Deep fry leeks in 350° oil for 2-3 minutes until brown and crisp. Drain on paper towels.

Fish

The Dish on Fish

I feel that fish offers you the greatest variety and versatility when it comes to cooking. For that reason, I offer a greater number of fish recipes in this book.

At Radnor Valley we have the ability to buy the freshest fish available. Beautiful yellowtail snappers, strawberry grouper, sushi grade tuna, and swordfish from a purveyor in Florida, who specializes in day boat catches (these are fisherman who bring their catch back to the docks everyday, opposed to those who fish for days or weeks at a time). We have local purveyors who have access to wonderfully fresh salmon, striped bass and skate from markets in Boston, New York and Maine.

This does not mean that you cannot find fresh fish for your home. Following are a few general tips you should follow when purchasing whole fish.

1) The fish should have a fresh, clean aroma.

2) The eyes should be clear and full, not sunken in.

3) Look for gills that are bright red, not brownish in color.

4) If possible, press the fish with a fingertip-it should feel firm and leave no visible finger imprint. However, quite often the fish market will not let you touch the fish.

5) At many markets they sell whole fish, as well as pre-cut fillets. Chances are the whole fish are fresher. Check them out with these tips and have them clean the fish for you.

6) Be flexible when buying fish. You may go to the market looking for salmon, but realize the red snapper is beautiful. Buy the best selection and then decide how you'd like to prepare it.

The following is information about some of the fish I have used in the upcoming recipes.

Atlantic Salmon

Basically, all the salmon available in today's market is farm raised. Large scale farming is done quite successfully in the United States, New Zealand, Norway, Canada, Chile, Ireland and Scotland. It is probably the most versatile fish around and lends itself to many flavors. At the restaurant we smoke it over mesquite wood, cure it pastrami-style, poach it, grill it, roll sushi and make burgers with it.

Occasionally, we are fortunate to get Copper River Sockeye salmon from Alaska and line caught Chinook salmon from the Pacific Northwest.

Tuna

One of my favorite dishes is a sashimi or seared rare steak of tuna. Yellowfin tuna is the most readily available. Be sure the color is a bright, shiny red and has a fresh smell. Avoid any tuna that is brownish in color or has a rainbow tint to it. After purchasing be sure to remove any dark colored meat, which is sometimes present along one side of the tuna. It is bitter when cooked. You may think you wouldn't enjoy eating a fish medium rare or rare, but the difference is amazing when it comes to tuna.

Chilean Sea Bass

The original species name is Patagonian Toothfish, but that made it an unattractive sell. Chilean sea bass is found throughout the Southern Hemisphere. It is a large, flaky fish that has a high oil content making it tender and moist (and virtually impossible to overcook). A little used fish a few years ago, Chilean bass is now one of the most popular in restaurants today. This popularity though will surely be to the disadvantage of the fish. After only a few years of use there are already signs of the depletion of the species due to overfishing. It may not be long before the availability of this fish is gone. That is always a disturbing fact to face. Maybe they should have kept the name Patagonian Toothfish!

Skate

This kite shaped fish is also called a ray. Generally, the term skate is used for the members of the species used for eating. "Ray" refers to those fished for sport, such as the giant manta ray. The skate has winglike pectoral fins that are the edible part of the fish. The flesh is white, firm and very sweet. It could be compared to that of a scallop. For years it was considered a trash fish in the United States, but it is now growing in popularity in many upscale restaurants. If you have the opportunity to try it, I highly recommend you do.

Striped Bass

There are two types of striped bass-farm raised and wild. Farm raised bass is readily available throughout the year. Wild striped bass has a very short season and is usually found along the East Coast. Wild bass is much larger and has a superior flavor to its farm raised counter part. Because of its availability the following recipes refer to farm raised striped bass.

*As I mentioned earlier, I love tuna. If you haven't noticed by now,
I also love mangoes. So, I serve the two together whenever I can.
I only recommend serving these dishes with sushi grade tuna.*

Sashimi of Tuna with Mango Glaze

SERVES 4

1 C. Fresh squeezed orange juice
1 tsp. Fresh ginger-minced
1 ½ C. Fresh mango-diced
2 T. Grapeseed oil
Salt and pepper to taste
1 Lb. Sushi grade tuna
2 C. Baby arugula-washed & dried

In a small saucepan add orange juice, ginger and 1 cup of the mango. Cook over medium high heat and reduce mixture by half. Place mixture in blender or food processor and blend until smooth. With blender on high slowly add grapeseed oil to thicken mixture. Season with salt and pepper.

Slice tuna in ¼ in. slices. Arrange tuna slices in center of a chilled plate. Top each plate with ½ C. baby arugula. Drizzle with mango glaze and garnish with remaining diced mango.

Ahi Tuna Carpaccio

SERVES 4

* 8 oz. Fresh Ahi tuna-sliced paper thin
1 T. Rice wine vinegar
1 T. Olive oil
Salt & fresh ground black pepper
1 Black truffle (optional)
Fresh ground parmesan

* If unable to slice tuna paper thin, place slices between two pieces of waxed paper and lightly pound thin.

Overlap tuna slices on serving platter. When ready to serve, sprinkle with rice wine, olive oil, salt and pepper. Freshly grate parmesan and black truffle over tuna. Serve tuna well chilled.

This is a great dish to serve as a first course. You can serve it on a bed of baby frisee or mixed greens that have been lightly tossed with balsamic vinaigrette. This dish is a great introduction for people who haven't tried tuna medium rare.

Ancho Chile Seared Tuna with Mango Tomato Salsa

SERVES 6

8 in. Fresh Ahi tuna loin-small diameter needed-about 1 ½ lbs.
3 T. Ancho chile powder-fresh ground
2 T. Fresh ground cumin seed
2 T. Fresh ground coriander seed
2 T. Kosher salt
2 T. Cracked black peppercorns
3 T. Grapeseed oil

Place a large sauté pan over high heat. Mix spices thoroughly and place in a flat pan. Pat tuna dry and roll in spices, coating tuna on all sides. Add oil to hot pan. Carefully place tuna in pan and sear for 2-3 minutes per side. Remove tuna from pan, it should remain rare to medium rare, and place in freezer for up to 2 hours. This will make the tuna easier to slice. Meanwhile, make the mango salsa.

Mango Tomato Salsa

2 C. Fresh mango-diced
1 C. Plum tomatoes-cored, seeded and diced
2 T. Diced roasted green chilies (canned)
1 T. Honey
1 T. Fresh squeezed lime juice
Salt and fresh ground pepper to taste

Toss all ingredients together and mix thoroughly. Slice tuna as thin as possible. Arrange 2 or 3 slices per serving on plate. Top with ½ cup of mango tomato salsa and serve.

Pan Seared Tuna Burgers with Wasabi Mayonnaise

MAKES 6 BURGERS

2 Lb. Fresh tuna steaks, skinless, dark colored flesh removed
2 T. Pickled ginger-minced
2 T. Rice wine vinegar
3 T. Soy sauce
2 T. Dijon mustard
* 1 T. Sriracha-asian hot sauce
2 T. Fresh cilantro-chopped
½ tsp. Salt
2 tsp. Sesame oil
1 T. Grapeseed oil

Chop tuna by hand until it resembles hamburger. Be sure to chop it evenly. Place tuna in a mixing bowl. In a separate bowl mix ginger, rice vinegar, soy sauce, mustard, sriracha, cilantro and salt. Add this mixture to chopped tuna and combine thoroughly.

Divide tuna into 6 equal amounts. Form tuna into 1 in. thick patties. Heat a large sauté pan over high heat and add sesame and grapeseed oils. Sear tuna burgers about 2 ½ minutes per side. This will give you a beautiful medium rare burger. Serve on your favorite roll with wasabi mayonnaise, sliced tomato and watercress.

Wasabi Mayonnaise

1 C. Mayonnaise
1 T. Wasabi paste (Japanese horseradish)
2 tsp. Snipped chives

Mix mayonnaise with wasabi and snipped chives. If you like it hotter, add more wasabi.

This simple preparation of Chilean bass will have everyone looking for more. This recipe is a perfect example of letting the true flavor of a fish come to life, without overpowering it. This one is a must!

Herb Marinated Grilled Chilean Sea Bass

. . . .

SERVES 4

4-8oz. Sea bass fillets-1-1 ½ in. thick
1 T. Fresh garlic-minced
1 tsp. Shallots-minced
1 T. Flat leaf parsley-chopped
2 T. Fresh basil-chopped
3 T. Extra virgin olive oil
Salt & fresh ground black pepper to taste
2 Lemons-halved

Score fish fillets on both sides in a cross hatch pattern, cutting into fish to a ¼ in. depth. In a small mixing bowl make a paste of the garlic, shallots, parsley, basil and olive oil. Season with salt and pepper.

Rub herb mixture on both sides of fish thoroughly. Place in a shallow platter, cover and refrigerate for 12-24 hours.

Prepare grill. Brush fish fillets with olive oil. Grill over medium high heat for 4-5 minutes per side. Remove from grill and serve. Squeeze lemon half over each fish fillet.

Pan Seared Chilean Sea Bass with Grilled Pineapple Chutney

. . . .

4-8oz. Chilean sea bass fillet
1 tsp. Ground cumin seed
1 tsp. Ground coriander seed
1 tsp. Ancho chile powder
1 tsp. kosher salt
2 T. Grapeseed oil
2 C. Grilled pineapple chutney (see recipe)

Mix cumin, coriander, chile powder and salt. Sprinkle bass fillets with spice mixture. Heat large sauté pan and add grapeseed oil. Sauté for 2 minutes on top side then turn. Finish in a 375° oven for 10 minutes or until desired doneness. Garnish with grilled pineapple chutney.

Grilled Pineapple Chutney

. . . .

MAKES ABOUT 2 CUPS

1 Medium pineapple-peeled, cored, cut into 1 in. thick rings
¼ C. Honey
¼ C. Soy sauce
2 T. Red bell pepper-diced
2 T. Red onion-diced
1 T. Cilantro-chopped
1 T. Fresh lime juice
Salt & ground pepper to taste

Mix soy sauce and honey together. Place sliced pineapple in mixing bowl and toss with honey-soy mixture. Grill pineapple over medium heat for about 30 seconds per side. Be careful, they will burn quickly due to honey glaze. Return to mixing bowl with reserved marinade.

When cool, dice pineapples and toss with remaining honey-soy marinade, bell pepper, red onion, cilantro and lime juice. Season with salt & pepper.

Halibut is another fish that is not used as often as it should be.
It has a firm, steak like texture that lends itself to many flavors.
This is one of my favorite halibut preparations.

Olive and Basil Roasted Halibut with Balsamic Vinegar Glaze

SERVES 4

¼ C. Calamata olives-pitted & chopped
1 T. Capers-chopped
2 T. Fresh basil-chopped
1 T. Fresh parsley-chopped
1 C. Japanese bread crumbs
3 T. Heavy cream
2 T. Dijon mustard
4 each 7-8 oz. Halibut fillets-1 in. thick

In a mixing bowl combine olives, basil, parsley, and bread crumbs. Set aside.

In a separate bowl mix heavy cream and mustard. Spread mustard mixture over top and sides of halibut. Place fish in a baking dish coated with non-stick cooking spray. Cover tops and sides of fish evenly with olive mixture.

Place fish in a preheated 450° oven for about 10-12 minutes or until fish is cooked through. Serve with balsamic vinegar glaze.

Many people think that reducing vinegar will give you an acidic
product. However, the reduction of a good balsamic vinegar gives
you a rich, sweet glaze. It's perfect for fish.

Balsamic Vinegar Glaze

⅓ C. Balsamic vinegar
2 T. Dry white wine
2 tsp. Shallots-minced
3 T. Unsalted butter

Place a small heavy-bottomed saucepan over high heat. Add balsamic vinegar, wine and shallots. Reduce mixture by half. Reduce heat to low. Stir in butter, 1 T. at a time until completely melted. Drizzle vinegar mixture over fish fillets.

It is very important that the salmon used for this preparation is extremely fresh. I think this dish holds a wonderful combination of flavors that may change the mind of a few people who never wanted to try salmon tartare.

Salmon and Greek Olive Tartare

SERVES 6-8

1 Lb Fresh Atlantic salmon fillet-skinned & boned
4 T. Calamata olives-pitted & chopped
1 T. Shallots-minced
1 ½ T. Fresh lemon thyme
2 tsp. Fresh parsley-chopped
1 tsp. Fresh chives-snipped
2 T. Fresh lemon juice
2 T. Olive oil
Fresh ground black pepper to taste
French bread slices-toasted

Place salmon in freezer for 20 minutes before serving so that it is thoroughly chilled. Meanwhile in a mixing bowl toss olives, shallots, lemon thyme, parsley, chives, lemon juice and olive oil.

Just before service, remove salmon from freezer and finely chop by hand. Toss salmon with olive mixture. Mix thoroughly. Serve salmon in the center of a chilled salad plate. Garnish with sliced cucumbers, lemon wedges, toasted french bread and fresh ground black pepper.

This dish may seem a little intimidating at first, but is not. However, this dish provides a stunning presentation that will certainly impress. Another option is to serve the salmon on a bed of mashed potatoes finished with chopped pickled ginger and wasabi.

Salmon and Crab Tempura with Toasted Curry Oil

SERVES 4

Tempura
1 Egg yolk
1 C. Ice water
1 C. Flour
* 1 tsp. Sriracha
Salt and pepper to taste

8-2 ½ oz. Slices Atlantic salmon (cut on bias to resemble sliced nova)
8 oz. Jumbo lump crabmeat
2 tsp. Pickled ginger-minced
1 T. Minced onion
1 tsp. Sesame oil
1 T. Soy sauce
1 Egg
¼ C. Heavy cream

Whisk ½ cup ice water with egg yolk. Slowly incorporate flour and remaining water. Season with sriracha, salt & pepper. Do not overmix, batter will toughen. Keep chilled.

Lightly pound out salmon medallions to give you a ¼ in. thick slice. Toss crabmeat with ginger, onion, sesame oil, soy sauce, egg and cream. Place 1 ounce of crab mixture in center of salmon and roll tightly to form a cylinder with both ends loosely sealed. Roll salmon in flour, coating well, then dip in tempura batter. Fry salmon in 350° oil for about 2 minutes until crisp. Remove from oil and drain on paper towels. Place salmon in a 400° oven for about 5 minutes to heat completely through. Remove from oven and slice salmon rolls in half on an angle. Present on a bed of toasted coconut rice (see recipe). Garnish each salmon and perimeter of plate with 2 tsp. of toasted curry oil.

Toasted Curry Oil

. . . .

1 tsp. Cumin seeds
1 tsp. Coriander seeds
1 tsp. Cardamom seeds
1 Clove
½ tsp. Fennel seed
1 tsp. Tumeric
½ tsp. Red pepper flakes
2 T. Fresh lime juice
½ C. Grapeseed oil

In a small sauté pan heat cumin, coriander, cardamom, clove, fennel, tumeric and red pepper flakes. Toast, stirring once, for about 3 minutes. Reduce heat to low. Add lime juice and grapeseed oil. Let simmer for 10 minutes. Remove from heat and let oil sit for 1 hour. Strain through cheesecloth or a fine sieve. Place in a squirt bottle to garnish. You can make larger batches if you want. Oil stays up to 1 month in refrigerator. It is good drizzled over grilled fish or chicken.

Pan Seared Atlantic Salmon with Coarse Mustard Sauce

. . . .

4-6oz Atlantic salmon fillet-skinned & boned
Coarse salt and fresh ground pepper to taste
2 T. Grapeseed oil
½ C. White wine
1 T. Shallots-minced
5 T. Unsalted butter
1 T. Coarse grain mustard
1 T. Dijon mustard
1 T. Fresh Tarragon-chopped

Season salmon with salt and pepper. Heat a large sauté pan and add grapeseed oil. Sear salmon fillets skinned side up for 3 minutes. Turn salmon and finish in a preheated 400° oven for an additional 6-8 minutes.

In a small saucepan bring white wine and shallots to a boil. Reduce to about 2 T. Lower heat and add 2 T. butter to pan, stirring constantly. As it melts add remaining butter 1 T. at a time. Remove from heat and stir in coarse mustard, dijon and tarragon. Stir until smooth. Serve atop each salmon fillet.

This dish is a variation to a cured salmon we serve at the club.
Instead of two days of curing to "cook" the fish we finish it on the grill.
This recipe is a nice change of pace for salmon.

Grilled Salmon Pastrami

SERVES 4

4-7 oz Atlantic salmon fillet-boneless & skinless
¼ C. Molasses-slightly warmed
1 T. Shallots
2 tsp. kosher salt
2 tsp. Cracked black pepper
2 tsp. Cracked coriander seed
2 tsp. Ground cumin seed
1 T. Lemon zest-minced

Place salmon fillets on a heavy baking sheet. Rub warmed molasses over both sides of the fish. Meanwhile, in a small mixing bowl combine remaining ingredients. Rub spice mixture over both sides of the fish. Cover fish with plastic wrap. Top with another baking sheet and weight with a heavy object. Refrigerate for at least 6 hours and up to 12.

Remove fish from pan and lightly pat dry. Grill over medium high heat for 4 minutes on each side. Serve with garlic mashed potatoes and grilled vegetables.

Garlic Roasted Salmon

· · · · · · · · · · · · · · · ·

SERVES 4

3 Garlic bulbs (follow directions for roasting garlic in roasted garlic vinaigrette)
2 T. Softened unsalted butter
½ C. Sour cream
2 T. Dijon mustard
Salt & pepper to taste
2 T. Japanese bread crumbs
4 each 7 oz. Atlantic salmon fillets-skinless & boneless

Place roasted garlic and butter in a food processor and blend until smooth. Add sour cream and mustard and puree until mixed thoroughly. Remove from processor and season with salt & pepper.

Place salmon on a baking sheet sprayed with non-stick cooking spray. Spread top of each salmon fillet with garlic mixture. Sprinkle with breadcrumbs. Bake fish uncovered in a preheated 375° oven for 10 minutes or until cooked through. Serve with fresh lemon. For a crisp top finish under broiler for 1 minute.

Grilled Atlantic Salmon, Arugula, Caramelized Onion-Tomato Coulis

· · · · · · · · · · · · · · · ·

SERVES 4

4 ea. 6 oz Atlantic salmon fillets
Grapeseed oil-to brush salmon
Salt and pepper
3 C. Fresh arugula (chiffonade cut)
1 T. Butter

Brush salmon fillets on both sides with grapeseed oil. Season with salt and pepper. Grill over medium high heat for approximately 4-5 minutes on each side. Heat large sauté pan and add butter. Quickly wilt arugula.

Garnish top of each fillet with wilted arugula. Serve on a bed of the onion tomato coulis.

Caramelized Onion-Tomato Coulis

. . . .

1 T. Olive oil
1 T. Fresh Garlic-chopped
½ C. Onions-diced
2 T. Balsamic vinegar
¼ C. Dry white wine
1 C. Crushed tomatoes (good quality canned)
2 T. Fresh basil-chopped
¼ tsp. Kosher salt
Fresh ground pepper to taste

In medium saucepan heat olive oil. Add garlic and onions and cook over medium high heat for 3-4 minutes or until caramelized. Add balsamic vinegar and white wine. Cook until liquid is reduced by half.

Add crushed tomatoes and simmer mixture for about 20 minutes. Remove from heat, add basil, salt and fresh ground pepper. Place in food processor or blender and puree until smooth. Can be prepared ahead of time and reheated. Makes about 1 ¼ cup.

Molasses Roasted Salmon with Carrot Ginger Sauce

SERVES 6

1 C. Fresh carrot juice
1 C. Fresh orange juice
2 T. Lemongrass (minced)
2 T. Ginger (minced)
* ½ T. Red curry paste
1 ½ T. Cornstarch
1 ½ T. Water
1 T. Chopped cilantro
2 T. Butter
¼ tsp. Kosher salt
6 T. Molasses
3 T. Sesame seeds (black and white)
6 ea. 8 oz. Salmon fillets
Grapeseed oil for sautéing
* *Available in oriental markets*

Add carrot juice, orange juice, lemongrass, ginger and red curry paste in a saucepan and simmer lightly for 10 minutes. Bring to a boil. Mix cornstarch and water together and add to sauce to thicken. Strain sauce through a fine sieve and return to saucepan.

Place over low heat and add butter and cilantro. Keep warm. Brush each salmon with 1 T. molasses and sprinkle with ½ T. sesame seeds.

Heat a large sauté pan and add 1 T. grapeseed oil. Sear salmon, sesame seed side first, for 2 minutes per side. Finish in a preheated 375° oven for 10-12 minutes. The molasses will give the fish a beautiful glaze. Serve salmon with carrot ginger sauce.

This fish goes well with a minted brown rice or roasted vegetable risotto. The butter can be omitted to make the dish more health conscious.

Macadamia Nut Roasted Atlantic Salmon
with Pickled Ginger Beurre Blanc

SERVES 4

4 each 6 oz. Atlantic salmon fillet-boneless & skinless
Salt & pepper to taste
1 T. Grapeseed oil
¾ C. Crushed macadamia nuts

Heat a non-stick sauté pan. Add grapeseed oil. Season salmon fillets with salt and pepper. Place salmon fillets in sauté pan skinned side up and cook for 3 minutes. Turn salmon and cook an additional 2 minutes. Remove from heat and top each salmon with equal amounts of macadamia nuts. Bake in 375° oven for 5 minutes or until done (depending on thickness of fish).

Pickled Ginger Beurre Blanc

5 T. Dry white wine
1 T. Rice wine vinegar
1 T. Pickled ginger-minced
1 tsp. Shallots-minced
4 T. Unsalted butter
1 T. Cilantro-chopped

Heat wine, vinegar, shallots and ginger in a heavy-bottomed saucepan. Bring to a boil and reduce by half. Add 2 T. butter and stir constantly. Lower heat and add remaining butter 1 T. at a time. When butter is almost melted completely remove from heat and stir until smooth. Add cilantro and serve over fish.

Here's a dinner you can have on the table in 15 minutes. Be sure to slice the fennel thin. You want it to be cooked through, but slightly crunchy. Serve on a bed of steamed cous cous and asparagus spears and you're set. This works great with chicken also.

Pan Seared Tuna with Braised Fennel and Artichokes

. . . .

SERVES 4

4-8oz Tuna steaks (1 ½ in. thick)
2 T. Olive oil
2 C. Fennel bulb, thin julienne
½ C. Red onion, thin julienne
2 tsp. Garlic, minced
1 C. Artichoke hearts, quartered
3 T. Balsamic vinegar
1 T. Fresh lemon juice
1 T. Flat leaf parsley-chopped
1 T. Fresh basil-chopped
Salt & pepper to taste

Place a large sauté pan over medium high heat. Season tuna on both sides with salt & pepper. Add olive oil to pan. Sear tuna for 2-3 minutes per side for medium rare. Remove from pan and keep warm.

In same pan add fennel, onion and garlic. Sauté over high heat for 2 minutes. Add artichoke hearts and cook additional 1 minute. Add balsamic vinegar and lemon juice, toss with fennel mixture and cook for 1 minute. Remove from heat and stir in parsley and basil. Season with salt and pepper. Serve tuna smothered with fennel mixture.

The sweetness of the balsamic vinegar goes extremely well with this delicate fish. This is one of the more popular presentations of skate at the restaurant.

Sautéed Skate Wing with Balsamic Vinegar Laced Beurre Blanc

. . . .

SERVES 4

4 T. Clarified butter
2 Lb Skate fillet-boneless, skinless - about 4 oz. each
Flour-to dredge skate, seasoned with salt & pepper
½ C. Balsamic vinegar
2 tsp. Shallots-minced
6 T. Unsalted butter
2 T. Capers
2 T. Italian flat parsley-chopped

Heat a large sauté pan and add 2 T. clarified butter. Dredge skate in seasoned flour on both sides. Add skate fillets, a few at a time, and cook for about 3 minutes per side. They should have a nice golden color. Remove fillets from pan and keep warm in a 200° oven. Cook remaining fillets, adding butter as needed.

When all fillets are cooked deglaze pan with balsamic vinegar and white wine. Add shallots and reduce mixture by half. Reduce heat and add butter 1 T. at a time, stirring constantly. Remove from heat as butter is finishing melting. Add capers and parsley, stir until smooth. Serve skate fillets topped with vinegar beurre blanc. This recipe works well with sole or chicken.

* Skate has a very similar taste to Dover sole or scallops. It can be found in some specialty fish markets.

Grilled Bass with Citrus Sauce

SERVES 4

1 Orange, lemon and lime
4-8 oz Striped bass fillet (boneless & skinless)
Salt & pepper to taste
2 T. Olive oil
¼ C. White wine
2 T. Balsamic vinegar
2 tsp. Shallots-minced
Reserved citrus juices
1 T. Capers
3 T. Unsalted butter

Cut rind and white pith from citrus. Carefully remove citrus segments from the fruit. Remove any seeds and dice segments. Set aside. Squeeze excess juice from inner skins and save.

Season bass with salt and pepper and brush with olive oil on both sides. Grill bass over medium high heat for about 3 minutes on each side. Keep warm while making citrus sauce.

In a heavy bottomed saucepan place white wine, balsamic vinegar and shallots over high heat and reduce mixture by half. Add reserved citrus juices and cook additional 1 minute. Lower heat and add butter 1 T. at a time, whisking constantly to keep sauce from separating. Remove from heat as butter is melting and stir in capers and reserved citrus segments. Spoon sauce over grilled bass fillets.

This is another beautiful presentation. Be careful when pounding the bass fillets, you don't want to tear the flesh. Serve this at your next special occasion. You're sure to get a great reaction. To save time the bass can be rolled up to a day ahead of time. There is that vinaigrette again – I can't help it – I love it.

Bass and Spinach Spirals with Toasted Coriander Seed-Orange Vinaigrette

SERVES 4

2 T. Unsalted butter
¼ C. Onions-finely diced
½ C. Shiitake mushrooms-finely diced
¼ C. Sundried tomatoes-finely diced
1 C. Fresh spinach-cut into a chiffonade
4-8 oz. Striped bass fillets-boneless & skinless
Flour for dredging fish
2 T. Grapeseed oil
2 T. Fresh lemon juice

In a medium saucepan melt butter over high heat. Add onions and shiitake mushrooms and cook for 3 minutes. Add sundried tomatoes and spinach and cook additional 1 minute or until spinach is just wilted.

Place bass fillets on flat surface and lightly pound them until fillet is fairly even. Spread spinach mixture over surface of bass fillets. Roll fillet from one end to the other, forming a spiral. Slice spirals in half, giving you two smaller spirals. Place toothpick through end of fillets to help keep their shape while cooking. Dredge fillets in flour seasoned with salt and pepper. Heat a medium sauté pan and add grapeseed oil. Sauté fish spirals for 2 minutes on each side. Sprinkle with lemon juice. Place pan in preheated 400° oven and finish cooking for additional 6-8 minutes. Remove toothpicks and serve with toasted coriander seed-orange vinaigrette. (see recipe in dressings chapter).

Cornmeal Crusted Trout with Pistachio Nut Butter

SERVES 4

¾ C. Cornmeal
¾ C. Flour, seasoned with salt & pepper
4 boneless trout, halved lengthwise, heads removed
3 T. Clarified butter
2 tsp. Shallots-minced
¾ C. Pistachio nuts-chopped
¼ C. Fresh squeezed lemon juice
5 T. Butter
2 T. Fresh basil-chopped
2 T. Fresh parsley-chopped

Mix cornmeal and flour together. Dip trout fillets in cornmeal mixture. Place a large sauté pan over medium high heat. Add 1 ½ T. clarified butter and cook half of trout in pan for about 2 minutes per side. Remove from pan and keep warm. Add remaining clarified butter and cook second batch of trout. Remove trout from pan and add shallots and pistachio nuts. Sauté for 1-2 minutes stirring constantly to brown nuts evenly. Add lemon juice and butter, stirring constantly so that butter thickens sauce and doesn't separate. Remove from heat and stir in basil and parsley. Place trout on a serving platter and spoon sauce over fish.

Here is a nice variation to your basic fried flounder.
If you like a little more zip in your tartar sauce, add extra wasabi.

Sesame Fried Flounder
with Wasabi Scented Tartar Sauce

SERVES 4

8 ea. 4-6 oz. Flounder fillets
Salt and pepper
Cornstarch for dredging fish
3 Lg. Eggs mixed with 1 T. water
1 ½ C. Japanese bread crumbs
¼ C. Black & white sesame seeds
Vegetable oil for frying

Season flounder with salt & pepper. In three separate dishes have ready the 1) cornstarch 2) eggwash 3) breadcrumbs mixed with sesame seeds. Dip each flounder fillet in cornstarch, eggwash and then breadcrumb mixture. You may need to press breadcrumbs into fish to help adhere.

In a heavy bottomed skillet heat about ¼ in. oil to 375°. Carefully add fish fillets to pan, a few at a time, and cook for 1 minute on each side. They should be golden brown. Remove fillets and place on paper towels to drain. Cook remaining fillets. Serve immediately with tartar sauce.

Wasabi Scented Tartar Sauce

¾ C. Mayonnaise
¼ C. Sweet pickle relish
1 T. Fresh lemon juice
1 T. Pickled ginger-minced
2 tsp. Wasabi paste

Combine all ingredients and refrigerate.

Grilled Red Snapper in Banana Leaf with Red Curry Lime Sauce

SERVES 4

4 ea. 7-9 oz. Boneless red snapper fillets
2 Garlic cloves
1 T. Fresh ginger
2 T. Fresh cilantro
½ tsp. Fresh ground black pepper
2 T. Soy sauce
4 Medium banana leaves
Grapeseed oil for brushing leaves

In a food processor add garlic, ginger, cilantro, pepper and soy sauce. Blend mixture thoroughly. Rub mixture over both sides of fish fillets. Refrigerate for 30 minutes and up to 1 hour.

Place banana leaves in a pot of boiling water for a few seconds to soften. With a sharp knife remove the thick spine of the leaf.

Place the shiny side of the leaf down. Brush leaf with oil. Set one fillet in center of each leaf. Fold over wide ends of leaf, overlapping at top. Turn over packages and fold over remaining ends to enclose. Secure packages with toothpicks where needed to make a neat parcel.

Grill over medium high heat for 4-5 minutes per side. Place each parcel on plate. Open leaf and serve with red curry-lime sauce.

Red Curry-Lime Sauce

2 T. Red curry paste
2 Garlic cloves
1 T. Ginger
2 T. Fresh cilantro
1 T. Sugar
¼ C. Fresh lime juice
2 T. Rice wine vinegar
¼ C. Chicken stock
Salt to taste

In a food processor combine red curry paste, garlic, ginger and cilantro. Puree into a paste. In a small saucepan add sugar, lime juice, rice vinegar and chicken stock. Bring mixture to a simmer. Stir in spice mixture. Season with salt. Serve in individual ramekins for dipping fish.

Oven Poached Red Snapper with Fennel and Plum Tomatoes

SERVES 4

1 ½ T. Olive oil
1 T. Garlic-minced
1 C. Onion-julienned
1 C. Fennel-core removed & julienned
5 C. canned plum tomatoes, rough chopped
½ C. White wine
10 Threads saffron
2 tsp. Fresh thyme
Salt and fresh ground pepper to taste
4-8 oz. Red snapper fillets, skinless & boneless

In a large sauté pan heat olive oil. Add onions, garlic and fennel and sauté until slightly soft, about 5 minutes. Add tomatoes, white wine and saffron and bring to a simmer. Stir in thyme and season with salt & pepper.

Spray a baking dish with non-stick cooking spray. Place fish fillets in dish in single layer. Pour warm sauce over fish. Cover with aluminum foil and bake in a preheated 400° oven for 15 minutes or until fish is cooked through. Fish should flake easily. Serve.

Char Grilled Swordfish with Citrus Salsa

SERVES 4

4-8 oz. Centercut swordfish steaks
2 tsp. Ancho chile powder
Salt & pepper
Olive oil
2 Oranges, skin & white pith removed, sectioned
1 Lemon, skin & white pith removed, sectioned
1 Lime, skin & white pith removed, sectioned
½ C. Plum tomatoes-seeded and diced
2 T. red onion-finely diced
2 T. Capers
1 T. Honey
1 T. Cilantro-chopped

Season both sides of swordfish with salt, pepper & chile powder. Brush with olive oil. Grill over medium high heat for 4-5 minutes per side.

Meanwhile, gently toss orange, lemon, lime, plum tomatoes, red onion, capers, honey and cilantro. Can be prepared up to 4 hours ahead.

Top grilled swordfish with citrus salsa and serve.

Poultry

A Few Words About Birds

. . . .

Chicken

Chicken is probably the ultimate triumph of mass production. However, this can lead to a certain mediocrity in flavor. Marinate chicken with fresh herbs and spices whenever possible. If you can, purchase free range chickens, I truly believe the extra expense is justified. Try it and decide for yourself.

Turkey

Turkey is becoming a great alternative to chicken, as well as veal. There are many more cuts available in the market today. Look for turkey breast cutlets. These are wonderful substitutes for any chicken or veal recipe in this book (and less expensive than veal and in many cases, chicken as well.) Once again, the free range turkey is superior to its mass produced counterpart. So you know, self basting turkeys are loaded with chemicals and sodium.

Duck

The most popular and readily available ducks in the market today are Long Island and Pekin ducks. However, these birds are very fatty. I prefer not to cook whole ducks. By the time the legs are done the breast is very dry and overcooked. I recommend cooking the breasts separately from the legs. At Radnor Valley, I prefer to use the breast of a Mallard duck. The breast is from the duck that is raised to produce foie gras. The duck breast, called a "magret," is much larger and juicier.

Ostrich

It has been touted as the premier red meat of the next century. That's right! Red meat. Most people just assume that an ostrich would be similar to a turkey or chicken. Ostrich has a deep, rich red color and looks and tastes very much like beef. Before you dismiss ostrich as a part of your diet, read the following facts.

1) Ostrich has 66% less fat than beef, 50% less than chicken

2) Less cholesterol than beef, chicken and pork

3) Higher in iron than beef

4) Raised throughout America as free range birds, without any chemicals or additives

5) Taste-it is wonderful and very versatile

More menus today are serving ostrich but as with many new trends, restaurants don't always do this fine bird justice by using inferior cuts and overcooking. Because the ostrich contains such a small amount of fat, it is highly recommended to be cooked no more than medium rare. Otherwise, you will experience a piece of meat that is not nearly as tender. I personally think it has great possibilities of becoming more popular. It is more expensive but allows the person who loves red meat the opportunity to enjoy it much more often. You can find many ranchers over the internet who will give you a plethora of information as well as the outlet to purchase portioned steaks by mail. I truly believe everyone should try it at least once.

I don't believe it gets any easier than this. You can prepare this up to a day ahead of time. In fact, the chicken is even better when prepared ahead. Be careful when making the beurre blanc. You don't want the butter to get too hot or it will separate.

Herb Mustard Roasted Chicken Breast with Roasted Red Pepper Beurre Blanc

8 ea. 3 oz. boneless chicken breast
⅓ C. Dijon mustard
2 T. Heavy cream
¾ C. Panko crumbs (Japanese coarse bread crumbs)
2 T. Fresh basil-chopped
2 T. Fresh parsley-chopped
1 T. Fresh chives-chopped

Toss chicken breast with mustard and heavy cream. Mix well. Mix bread crumbs and fresh herbs. Dredge each chicken breast in bread crumb mixture. Bake chicken breast in 375° preheated oven for 10-12 minutes. Serve chicken topped with roasted red pepper beurre blanc.

Roasted Red Pepper Beurre Blanc

½ C. Dry white wine
1 T. Shallots-minced
6 T. Unsalted butter
3 T. Roasted red peppers-chopped

Heat wine in a heavy bottomed saucepan with shallots and bring to a boil. Reduce wine by half. Add 2 T. of butter and stir. Lower heat and add butter 1 T. at a time. When butter is almost completely melted, remove from heat and stir until smooth. Add roasted peppers and season with salt and pepper. Serve immediately.

Grilled Chicken with Roasted Peppers, Arugula and Greek Olive Vinaigrette

SERVES 4

10 Calamata olives-pitted
2 tsp. Fresh thyme leaves
1 T. Dijon mustard
2 tsp. Garlic-minced
¼ C. Balsamic vinegar
½ C. Olive oil
8 each 3 oz. boneless, skinless chicken breast-brushed with olive oil, salt and pepper to taste
1 C. Roasted red peppers
4 C. Arugula leaves-rinsed well and dried

In a food processor, place olives, thyme, mustard, garlic and vinegar and blend until smooth. With machine running slowly incorporate olive oil until dressing is emulsified. Season with salt and pepper.

Grill chicken breasts over medium high heat for 3-4 minutes per side, depending on thickness of chicken. Divide the arugula and roasted peppers between 4 plates. Place 2 chicken breasts atop each. Drizzle with greek olive vinaigrette and serve.

A nice alternative to fried chicken.

Pistachio Fried Chicken Breast

SERVES 4

8 ea. 3oz. Boneless chicken breasts (pounded to ¼ in. thickness)
¾ C. Flour-seasoned with salt and pepper
¾ C. Milk
2 Eggs
1 C. Finely ground pistachio nuts
1 C. Japanese bread crumbs
Peanut oil for pan frying

Place seasoned flour in a bowl. In a separate bowl mix milk and eggs. In a third bowl toss pistachios and breadcrumbs.

In a heavy bottomed Dutch oven heat about 1in. of oil to 350°. Lightly dredge chicken in flour, then egg mixture, then breadcrumb mixture. Shake off any excess nut mixture.

Pan fry chicken breasts for 2-3 minutes on each side until nicely browned and cooked through. Drain chicken on paper towels and serve. Drizzle with honey before serving for a little added flavor.

This recipe is a little bit of work but worth the effort. You can also freeze any extra dumplings before the cooking process. Cook an additional 5 minutes from frozen state. Ask your butcher to grind your chicken, if no grinder is available.

You can serve these dumplings in chicken soup or tossed with an assortment of vegetables for an original stir fry (if serving in soup, don't sauté the dumplings).

Pan Roasted Chicken Dumplings with Thai Peanut Sauce

1 Lb. Ground chicken breast & thigh meat
1 T. Fresh ginger-minced
1 T. Green onion - minced
2 T. Garlic-minced
1 Egg white
2 T. Cornstarch
2 tsp. Salt
2 T. Soy sauce
1 T. Sesame oil
¼ tsp. White pepper
20 Wonton Skins
1 Egg mixed with 1 T. water (eggwash)
Grapeseed or olive oil as needed

Mix ground chicken with ginger, green onion, garlic, egg white, cornstarch, salt, soy sauce, sesame oil and white pepper. Mix thoroughly. Place 1 T. of chicken mixture to one side of skin. Brush opposite side of skin with egg wash. Fold skin over chicken mixture to form a dumpling. Press sides of dumpling tightly, removing any air pockets. If there is any excess wonton skin, cut away. Chill dumplings after preparation.

In a 10 qt. pot, boil water and add 2 T. oil. Cook dumplings for 10 minutes, stirring occasionally, to prevent sticking. Remove dumplings and rinse under cold water. Toss with grapeseed oil to prevent sticking together.

In a large sauté pan, heat 2 T. grapeseed oil. Sauté dumplings, a few at a time, for 1-2 minutes on each side until skins are lightly crisp. Remove from pan and serve with thai peanut sauce for dipping.

Thai Peanut Sauce

. . . .

2 T. Sesame Oil
⅔ C. Onion-chopped fine
1 T. Minced Garlic
* 2 T. Red curry paste
1 tsp. Ground cumin seed
1 tsp. Ground coriander seed
1 tsp. Paprika
1 ½ C. Unsweetened canned coconut milk (stirred well)
½ C. Chicken stock
¾ C. Finely ground unsalted, roasted peanuts
* 1 T. Siracha (asian hot sauce)
2 T. Soy sauce
¼ C. Brown sugar
2 T. Rice wine vinegar
1 T. Lime juice
Available in Chinese markets

Heat sesame oil in a heavy bottomed saucepan. Sauté onion, garlic and ginger for about 3 minutes, stirring occasionally. Stir in red curry paste, cumin, coriander and paprika. Mix well. Add coconut milk, stirring to keep it from sticking. Add chicken stock and simmer for about 10 minutes or until slightly reduced. Add peanuts and cook until thickened. Stir in soy sauce, sugar, vinegar and lime juice. Remove from heat. This sauce can be made days ahead and freezes rather well.

Sautéed Chicken Breasts with Green Peppercorn Sauce

SERVES 4

8 ea. 3 oz. Boneless, skinless chicken breast halves
2 T. Olive oil
1 T. Shallots-minced
2 C. Shiitake mushrooms-stems removed and sliced
½ C. Dry white wine
1 C. Heavy cream
1 T. Worcestershire
1 ½ T. Green peppercorns
1 T. Fresh basil

Place a large sauté pan over medium high heat. Season chicken with salt and pepper and dredge in flour. Add olive oil to pan and cook chicken on both sides until lightly browned. Remove from pan and finish on a baking sheet in a preheated 400° oven for about 5 minutes.

In same sauté pan add shallots and mushrooms and sauté for 2-3 minutes. Add white wine, heavy cream, worcestershire and green peppercorns. Render mixture for about 5 minutes, sauce should be slightly thickened. Stir in fresh basil and serve atop sautéed chicken breast.

Greek Chicken Cheesesteak

4-3oz. Chicken breast-pounded very thin
2 tsp. Fresh garlic
2 tsp. Fresh basil
2 T. & 2 tsp. Olive oil
½ C. Feta cheese
3 T. Calamata olives-pitted & chopped
½ C. Plum tomatoes-seeded & chopped
2-10 in. Steak rolls

In a mixing bowl add chicken, garlic, basil and 2 T. olive oil. Mix well and let stand refrigerated 1-4 hours.

Heat a medium sauté pan and add 2 tsp. olive oil. Sear chicken breast for 1 minute on each side. Remove from pan and slice chicken into thin strips. Place back in pan and finish cooking chicken through-about 2 minutes. Add feta cheese, olives and plum tomatoes. Heat mixture through and serve on warm steak rolls.

Sautéed Chicken Breast with Caper Chevre Beurre Blanc

8 ea. 3 oz. Chicken breast fillets-pounded thin
Flour for dredging, seasoned with salt and pepper
2 T. Grapeseed oil
½ C. White wine
2 tsp. Shallots-minced
3 T. Unsalted butter-cubed
3 oz. Softened Chevre
3 T. Roasted peppers-chopped fine
2 T. Capers
2 T. Fresh basil-chopped

In a large sauté pan, heat grapeseed oil. Dredge chicken in flour and sear for 2 ½ minutes on each side. Remove from pan and keep warm in a 200° oven. Drain oil and deglaze pan with white wine and shallots. Reduce mixture by half and lower heat to a simmer. Stir in butter, a tablespoon at a time, to keep from separating. When butter is almost melted remove from heat, stir in chevre, roasted peppers, capers and basil. Continue stirring until all butter and chevre is incorporated into sauce. You may have to heat sauce slightly at this time. Serve sauce over chicken breasts.

Crispy Coconut Chicken

1 T. Garlic-minced
1 T. Ginger-minced
2 tsp. Red curry paste
1 T. Heavy cream
4-8 oz. Chicken breast-boneless, skinless and halved
Flour for dredging chicken-seasoned with salt & pepper
3 Eggs mixed with 1 T. water
2 C. Shredded coconut
3 T. Clarified butter
Diced mangos for garnish

In a mixing bowl combine garlic, ginger, red curry paste and heavy cream. Toss chicken breast with spice mixture and let sit 2 hours. Dredge chicken in flour, and then dip in egg wash, letting excess drip off. Dip chicken in coconut, pressing coconut into chicken.

In a large sauté pan heat clarified butter. Sauté chicken breast for about 3 minutes per side. Transfer chicken to a preheated 350° oven until cooked through, about 6-8 minutes. Garnish with diced mangos.

Everybody loves roast chicken. Try this exciting recipe next time.
The pomegranate molasses along with the ginger and orange imparts
a unique flavor to the roast chicken.

Orange and Ginger Roasted Chicken

5-6 lb. Roasting chicken
2 Navel oranges-quartered
2 T. Orange zest-removed from quartered oranges
4 T. Ginger-minced
Fresh ground black pepper and salt
4 T. Butter
* ⅓ C. Pomegranate molasses (honey can be substituted)
2 T. Fresh ground coriander seed
¾ Cup Fresh squeezed orange juice
* *Available in gourmet food stores*

Rinse chicken and pat dry. Rub orange zest and half of ginger on outside of chicken. Season with salt and pepper and 1 T. coriander. Place quartered oranges inside cavity of chicken.

In a small saucepan combine butter, pomegranate molasses, orange juice and remaining coriander seed. Heat gently. Roast chicken in center of oven, basting chicken with juice mixture 4-6 times during roasting. Cook chicken 2-2 ½ hours or until meat thermometer inserted in meaty part of thigh registers 170°.

Let chicken stand 10 minutes before carving. If wanted, a gravy can be made by straining remaining juice mixture, bringing to a boil and thickening with cornstarch-water mixture.

This is certainly a different type of presentation for duck. You will probably need a meat grinder for this recipe (the duck breast you purchase will most likely be frozen. You will need to remove the skin and grind it). If duck is unavailable, try the same recipe with ground turkey.

Pan Roasted Southwestern Duck Cakes

SERVES 6

1 T. & 2 T. Olive oil
⅓ C. Red bell pepper-diced
⅓ C. Yellow bell pepper-diced
½ C. Onion-diced
2 T. Garlic-minced
¼ C. Dry white wine
3 Lbs. Skinless duck breast-ground
1 T. Ancho chile powder-freshly ground
2 tsp. Ground cumin seed
2 tsp. Ground coriander seed
2 T. Cilantro-chopped
¼ C. Worcestershire sauce
½ tsp. Salt
1 tsp. tabasco
1 C. Ground pistachios

Garnish
8 oz. Crumbled chevre
1 Pt. Teardrop tomatoes
Caramelized red onion vinaigrette

Heat a medium sauté pan and add 1 T. olive oil. Add red and yellow pepper, onion and garlic. Sauté for 2 minutes. Add white wine and cook additional 1 minute. Remove from heat and set aside.

In a large mixing bowl toss duck with chile powder, cumin, coriander, cilantro, worcestershire, salt and tabasco. Add pepper-onion mixture and blend thoroughly.

Form duck into 12-4oz. cakes. Place a large sauté pan over medium high heat. Add 1 T. of olive oil to pan and cook duck cakes, a few at a time, for 1 minute on each side. Add remaining olive oil, if needed, and cook remaining duck cakes.

Sprinkle duck cakes with pistachio nuts and place in a 400° oven for 12-15 minutes. Remove from oven and keep warm. Serve 2 cakes each sprinkled with teardrop tomatoes and crumbled chevre. Finish drizzled with caramelized red onion vinaigrette. (See recipe in Dressing Chapter)

The following three recipes give you a nice array of choices for duck breast. They are all rather light for duck. When scoring the duck skin, it may help to freeze the breast for 15 minutes. This will harden the skin and make it easier to score and keep you from cutting the flesh.

Honey Lacquered Duck Breast

SERVES 4

4 ea. 8 oz. Boneless duck breasts
¾ c. Honey
½ C. Port wine or burgundy
1 T. Fresh ginger-minced
2 each Allspice
1 each Star anise
8 each Black peppercorns
1 T. Orange zest
Salt and pepper to taste

Trim any excess fat from the duck breast. With a sharp knife make slits in the skin about ¼ in. apart, making a cross hatch or diamond pattern. This will allow for more of the fat to be rendered from the skin and give you a nice golden, crisp skin.

Combine the honey and port in a small saucepan and reduce by half. Add all spices and orange zest. Simmer additional 5 minutes. Let cool to room temperature and then strain.

Place a large sauté pan over medium high heat. Season duck with salt and pepper. When pan is very hot, place the duck, skin side down, in the pan. Reduce heat slightly and cook for about 6-8 minutes or until skin is golden brown. Carefully turn duck and cook additional minute. Drain excess fat from pan. Brush duck breasts liberally with honey mixture. Place in a preheated 450° oven. Cook for 3-4 minutes to medium rare. Duck should have a nice shiny finish. Remove from pan and let stand 2 minutes. Slice duck breast thin and drizzle with remaining glaze from pan. Serve as entrée or in your favorite salad.

Crisp Duck Breast, Sundried Cherry Glaze, Ginger Scented Cous Cous, Frizzled Leeks

. . . .

6 ea. 8 oz. Boneless duck breasts
Salt and Pepper to taste

Place a large sauté pan over high heat. Score the skin of the duck breast in a cross hatch pattern. This will allow for more of the fat to be rendered and give you a crispy skin. Pat duck breasts dry. Season with salt and pepper. Place duck in pan, skin side down, and reduce heat to medium high. Cook for 6-8 minutes or until skin is evenly browned. Carefully pour off excess duck fat. Turn duck and cook additional 2-3 minutes. Remove from pan and keep warm.

Sundried Cherry Glaze
1 T. Fresh ginger-minced
2 tsp. Shallots-minced
2 C. Apple juice
½ C. Veal demiglace
½ C. Honey
3 T. Raspberry Vinegar
2 C. Shiitake Mushrooms-stems removed and sliced
¾ C. Dried cherries
1 T. Fresh thyme leaves

After removing duck, drain any fat and add ginger, shallots, apple juice, demiglace, honey and raspberry vinegar. Cook over high heat for 5 minutes. Add mushrooms, cherries and thyme and continue cooking until sauce is a light, syrupy glaze. Slice duck breast thin and quickly toss with glaze to coat evenly.

Garnish
2 Leeks (white only-julienned)

Place leeks in 350° fryer. Cook until browned and crisp, stirring occasionally. Remove and drain on paper towel.

To Serve – Place cous cous (see recipe in Pasta & Grains chapter) in corner of plate. Fan duck breast around plate. Ladle sauce over duck. Top with frizzled leeks.

Pan Seared Duckling Breast, Watermelon-Cantaloupe Salsa, Toasted Barley Salad

. . . .

Duckling
6 ea. 8 oz Duck breast
2 tsp. Ancho chile powder (freshly ground)
Kosher salt and pepper to taste

Place a large sauté pan over high heat. Meanwhile, score the skin of the duck breast in a cross hatch pattern. Be careful not to cut into the flesh. Pat duck breast dry. Season duck with Ancho chile powder, salt and pepper. Place duck in pan, skin side down, and reduce heat to medium high. Cook for 6-8 minutes or until skin is evenly browned. Carefully pour off excess duck fat. Turn duck and cook to desired temperature - about 2 minutes for medium rare. Remove duck from pan and let stand for 2 minutes. Slice duck thinly. Serve hot.

Watermelon-Cantaloupe Salsa
¾ C. Seedless watermelon-diced
¾ C. Yellow watermelon-diced-seeds removed
¾ C. Cantaloupe-seeded & diced
¾ C. Yellow tomatoes-skinned, seeded & diced
1 T. Jalapeno pepper-seeded & finely diced
1 T. Honey
1 T. Fresh lime juice
1 T. Cilantro-chopped

Toss all ingredients and let stand refrigerated for at least 1 hour.

Garnish
9 oz. Assorted baby greens
2 T. Olive oil
2 T. Fresh orange juice
2 T. Balsamic vinegar
Salt & pepper to taste

Toss greens with oil, vinegar and orange juice. Season with salt and pepper.

To Serve – Place toasted barley salad (see Pasta & Grains Chapter) in center of plate. Arrange sliced duck breast around barley. Sprinkle duck with watermelon salsa. Top barley with baby greens.

Here's another quick, easy dinner that can be prepared in no time.
You can cook the proscuitto up to a week ahead. Just crumble and
refrigerate in an airtight container.

Proscuitto Roasted Turkey Cutlet with Tomato Chutney

10 Slices proscuitto-paper thin
¾ C. Japanese breadcrumbs
8-4 oz. Turkey breast cutlet
⅓ C. Dijon mustard
2 T. Heavy cream
½ C. Parmesan cheese
3 T. Basil-chopped
2 T. Parsley-chopped

Bake proscuitto on a baking sheet for 10 minutes at 375° or until very crisp. Let cool and crumble. Toss proscuitto with breadcrumbs, parmesan, basil and parsley.

Toss turkey with mustard and heavy cream to coat evenly. Dredge each turkey cutlet in herb mixture. Bake at 400° for 10 minutes or until cooked through. Serve with tomato chutney.

Tomato Basil Chutney

1 T. Olive oil
2 tsp. Fresh garlic-minced
¼ C. White wine
2 C. Diced plum tomatoes (good quality, canned)
1 T. Fresh basil-chopped

In a medium saucepan heat olive oil. Add garlic and sauté for 1 minute. Add white wine and cook additional 2 minutes. Add tomatoes and basil and heat through. Can be made up to 3 days ahead.

Growing up, meatloaf was always my favorite. In fact, it still is. When friends tell me "I can't cook for a chef," I tell them to make me meatloaf. The following is a nice change of pace to this old standby.

Turkey Spinach Meatloaf

2 T. Olive oil
1 ½ C. Onion-finely diced
3 T. Garlic-minced
¼ C. Dry white wine
¼ C. Worcestershire sauce
2 T. Tomato paste
½ C. Ketchup
¼ C. Dijon mustard
1 tsp. Thyme leaves
2 tsp. Tabasco
2 lbs. Ground turkey, lean
1 ½ C. Breadcrumbs
2 Eggs, beaten
¼ C. Parmesan
2 T. Parsley, chopped
3 T. Fresh basil, chopped
2 C. Cooked, chopped spinach (squeezed to remove moisture)
1 ½ tsp. Salt

Heat a large sauté pan and add olive oil. Sauté onions and garlic for 5 minutes until lightly browned. Add white wine and cook additional 1 minute. Stir in worcestershire, tomato paste, ketchup, mustard, thyme and tabasco. Cook for 1-2 minutes. In a large mixing bowl add turkey, breadcrumbs, eggs, parmesan, parsley, basil, spinach and salt. Mix well. Add onion mixture and combine thoroughly. Form turkey mix into an oval loaf. Cook in a preheated 350° oven for 1 hour or until a meat thermometer placed in the center of loaf reads 160°. Serve with tomato basil chutney or top with marinara sauce and melted provolone.

You may never want to eat beef hamburgers again!

All White Meat Turkey Burgers with Ancho Chile Mayonnaise

. . . .

3 Lbs. Ground turkey breast
1 Head garlic-brushed with olive oil
3 T. olive oil
3 T. Worcestershire sauce
2 tsp. Kosher salt
2 tsp. Tabasco sauce
2 tsp. Thyme

Wrap garlic in foil and roast in a preheated 400° oven for about 45 minutes, or until soft. When cool, cut very top of garlic head with a sharp knife. Squeeze roasted garlic from head.

Combine turkey with garlic, olive oil, worcestershire, salt, tabasco and thyme. Be sure ingredients are well incorporated. Form 7 oz. patties about ¾ in. thick. Grill over medium heat for about 6-8 minutes to a side. Turkey burgers take longer to cook than beef, so they must be cooked over a lower heat.

Ancho Chile Mayonnaise

. . . .

1 C. Mayonnaise
2 tsp. Ancho chile powder
Tabasco sauce to taste
2 tsp. Fresh lime juice

Combine mayonnaise, chile powder, tabasco and lime juice. Stir. Can be made 2-3 days ahead.

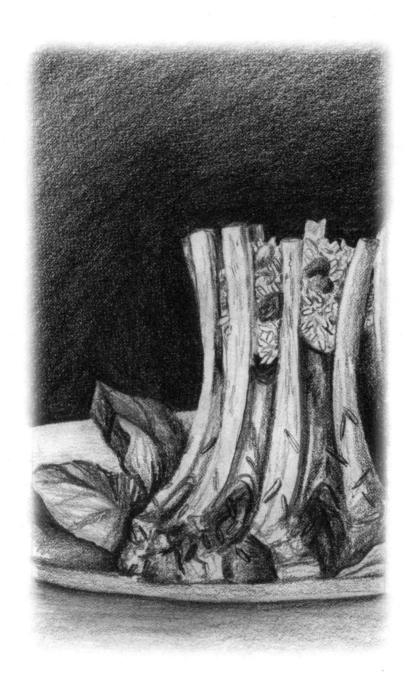

Meats

Here's the Rub on Beef

Beef

In general, mass production has also had its affect on the flavor of beef today. However, there are butchers and supermarkets out there who pride themselves on carrying good, quality beef. It just may take a few visits to find out. There are 3 USDA grades-select, choice and prime. Try to purchase choice or prime. There is also certified angus beef which I will discuss shortly. Generally, the higher the grade, the more tender and flavorful it will remain after cooking. You want to select meat that is well marbled with fat.

Certified Angus Beef

The Certified Angus Beef Program was formed in 1978 by the American Angus Association. To date, this is the largest beef cattle registry in the United States. The program was formed when the USDA lowered its standards for choice and prime grades of meat. The requirements set by the Certified Angus Program are so strict that only 6 of 100 cattle pass the stringent test. There is a debate among chefs on whether Certified Angus Beef is truly the best beef available. I believe that it offers a chef a consistent product in regards to flavor and tenderness. There are some markets that carry this product and be ready to pay a heftier price. As I have mentioned before, try it and decide for yourself. Be wary, however, for stores that offer sound-a-likes such as Black Angus, Angus Beef and USDA Certified Black Angus.

As you will notice, I did not spend a lot of time writing recipes for steaks. I prefer to simply grill steaks with a dry rub of spices or a roasted garlic marinade. I love to finish the steaks with a sprinkle of fleur de sel (French sea salt).

A dry rub is a blend of fresh or dry herbs applied to the outside of uncooked steaks. These rubs can also contain a small amount of oil, mustard or fresh garlic. Marinades for beef should always contain an acidic ingredient, such as wine or balsamic vinegar, if being used for tenderizing. A small amount of oil added to the marinade will also help it adhere to the meat better. My favorite marinade is a simple mix of roasted garlic, balsamic vinegar, worcestershire sauce, olive oil and fresh ground black pepper. I will now offer what I hope is some helpful information on lamb and veal.

Lamb

Lamb has become increasingly popular. Improved farm raising techniques has given lamb increased flavor and tenderness. New Zealand and Australia are very large producers of lamb and are providing a consistently better product. However, domestic lamb is considered by many a superior product, and oddly enough is more expensive than its imported counterpart. There are butcher shops who sell totally cleaned racks of New Zealand and Australian racks of lamb frozen. The recipes in this book use domestic and imported lamb. When purchasing a leg of lamb, ask your butcher to bone, roll and tie it for you (unless you are going to stuff it yourself, then just have him bone it). Be sure to ask for the bones, cut into 4 inch pieces, for making stock. **The "Leg of Lamb stuffed with Broccoli Raab and Feta" is a must try for lamb lovers.**

Veal

The most prevalent veal on the market today is milk fed veal-otherwise known as formula fed or natured. It has a smooth texture with light pink color. Grass fed veal is from older calves and has a grainy texture and much darker color. Be sure when buying cutlets they come from the leg or loin and that they are sliced thin. When purchasing chops, I prefer the rib chops over the loin. There may be more fat but it is easily removed after cooking and gives you a juicier piece of veal. When purchasing veal chops, you can expect to pay anywhere from $11-$17 a pound, depending on the quality and size of the cut. A new product to look for in the near future-veal bacon-25% less fat and 50% fewer calories. It cooks very similar to pork bacon and is rather tasty.

Cumin Roasted Rack of Lamb with Balsamic Vinegar Roasted Onions

SERVES 2

½ C. Japanese Breadcrumbs
2 tsp. Ground cumin
1 tsp. Ground coriander seed
2 tsp. Garlic-minced
1 T. Olive oil
1 ea. 1 ¼-1 ½ lbs. Lamb rack-frenched & trimmed of fat
1 T. Dijon mustard
Salt and pepper to taste

In a mixing bowl combine breadcrumbs, cumin, coriander, garlic, and olive oil. Season lamb with salt and pepper and rub meat side of lamb with dijon mustard. Spread breadcrumb mixture evenly over mustard. Roast lamb in a preheated 475° oven, breadcrumb side up, for 5 minutes. Reduce heat to 400° and cook additional 10 minutes or until a meat thermometer placed in center of meat registers 125° for medium rare. Let lamb stand for 5 minutes before serving. Cut lamb between rib bones and serve.

Balsamic Vinegar Roasted Onions

2 Lg. Red onions
1 T. Garlic-minced
¼ C. balsamic vinegar
2 T. Olive oil
2 T. Worcestershire sauce
1 tsp. Thyme
¼ tsp. Salt
Fresh ground black pepper to taste

Slice onions in half, leaving root end attached. Peel off skin. In a small baking dish mix garlic, balsamic vinegar, olive oil, worcestershire sauce, thyme, salt and pepper. Add onions and toss thoroughly with marinade. Let sit for up to 3 hrs.

Bake onions in a preheated 375° oven for 1 hour or until a knife inserts in the center easily. Remove onions from oven and place in a serving dish. Drizzle onions with some of the baking liquid. Wonderful with grilled steaks too.

*At Radnor Valley we serve this dish with the New Zealand rack of baby
lamb. It is easily one of the most popular dishes on the menu.
Try it and you will see why.*

Sesame Grilled Lamb Chops with Oriental Black Bean Demiglace

. . . .

SERVES 4

⅓ C. Soy sauce
2 T. Worcestershire sauce
¼ C. Honey
1 T. Ginger-minced
½ T. Garlic-minced
2 t. Sriracha (asian hot sauce) *
2 T. Sesame oil
16-3 oz. Australian or domestic lamb rib chops-frenched
1 C. Veal demiglace
2 tsp. Fermented black beans-rinsed & chopped

* If you cannot find sriracha, you can substitute Tabasco, but only use ½ tsp.

Place soy sauce, worcestershire, honey, ginger, garlic and sriracha in food
processor and puree until smooth. Slowly incorporate sesame oil in marinade.
Reserve ¼ cup marinade. Toss lamb chops with remaining marinade and let sit up
to 4 hours. Remove chops from marinade and grill over medium high heat for 3
minutes on each side for medium rare. Heat veal demiglace with ¼ cup reserved
marinade and fermented black beans. Serve lamb chops with black bean demiglace.
Sweet potato risotto (a mixture of risotto and mashed sweet potatoes) goes very
well with this dish. An additional garnish of crispy yams could also be used.

If you can't get the baby lamb chops for this recipe, you can substitute domestic rib chops, which will average around 3 or 4 oz. each. The marinade will make an already tender product melt in your mouth.

Ancho Chile Grilled Baby Lamb Chops

SERVES 2

1 ½ T. Ancho chile powder
1 T. Ground coriander seed
1 T. Ground cumin seed
1 T. Brown sugar
2 T. Balsamic vinegar
1 tsp. Black pepper
1 tsp. Salt
1 T. Olive oil
8 each-Double cut baby lamb chops, about 3 oz each

In a small bowl combine spices, sugar, vinegar and oil. Rub mixture over lamb chops, refrigerate, and let marinate for 6-12 hours.

Place lamb chops over medium high grill and cook for 2-3 minutes per side for medium rare. Serve with mashed potatoes or risotto.

The following two recipes are fairly easy preparations of a dish rarely cooked in the home kitchen. Ask your butcher to french the rack (this will give you a clean looking product) and to remove the chine bone (this will allow you to cut down between each chop).

Herb Mustard Roasted Rack of Lamb

. . . .

SERVES 2

1 each-Rack of lamb 1 ¼-1 ½ lbs., frenched, 8 ribs
Salt and pepper to season
1 T. Olive oil
1 tsp. Fresh garlic-minced
1 tsp. Shallots-minced
2 T. Dijon mustard
1 T. Heavy cream
⅓ C. Panko crumbs *
1 T. Fresh rosemary-chopped
1 T. Fresh thyme leaves
1 tsp. Fresh parsley-chopped
1 tsp. Fresh basil-chopped

* Japanese coarse breadcrumbs-available in gourmet markets

In a small pan heat olive oil. Season lamb with salt and pepper. Sear lamb in pan on both sides and ends for about 4 minutes. Be sure to brown evenly. Remove from pan and drain any excess fat. Add garlic and shallots and sauté for 1 minute. Remove from heat and stir in mustard and heavy cream. Spread mustard mixture on meat side of lamb. Toss breadcrumbs with rosemary, thyme, parsley and basil. Spread herb breadcrumbs evenly over mustard. Bake in a preheated 475° oven for 5 minutes, reduce heat to 400° and cook additional 10 minutes or until a meat thermometer reads 125° for med rare. Remove from oven and let stand for 5 minutes. Cut between each bone and serve.

Roast Leg of Lamb Stuffed with Broccoli Raab and Feta Cheese

1 ½ Lb. Broccoli raab, large stems removed and coarse chopped
1 T. Shallots, minced
2 T. Olive oil
1 C. Feta cheese-crumbled
5 lbs. Boneless leg of lamb, boned, butterflied and trimmed well
1 T. Rosemary
1 C. Dijon mustard
1 T. Garlic-minced
2 T. Worcestershire sauce
1 ½ C. Burgundy
2 C. Veal stock
2 T. Water mixed with 1 T. cornstarch
2 T. Coarse mustard-optional

Wash broccoli raab and drain. Place raab in a large saucepan with a small amount of liquid. Steam for 1-2 minutes until wilted. Refresh raab under cold water and squeeze dry. Add olive oil and shallots to sauté pan and cook over medium heat for 2 minutes. Add raab and cook additional 1 minute. Remove from pan and let cool. Stir in feta cheese.

Lay lamb on work surface with boned side up. Season with salt and pepper. Spread feta cheese mixture evenly over surface of lamb. Beginning at the short side of lamb, roll up in a jelly roll fashion. Tie lamb every 2 inches with butcher's twine. It should resemble a somewhat uniform shape that will improve in appearance when cooked. Rub outside of lamb with rosemary, mustard, worcestershire and garlic. Place lamb in a roasting pan and cook in a preheated 350° oven, allowing 20 minutes of cooking time per pound or until meat thermometer registers 130° for medium rare. Remove lamb from pan and let stand 10-15 minutes before carving.

Place roasting pan over medium heat, skimming as much fat as possible from the pan juices. Deglaze pan with burgundy, scraping away any browned bits from roasting pan. Cook wine until reduced by half. Strain mixture thru a fine sieve into a medium saucepan. Add veal stock and bring mixture to a boil. Reduce mixture to about 1 ½ cups. While simmering whisk in cornstarch mixture and cook additional 2-3 minutes. Add coarse mustard. Season with salt and pepper.

Remove strings from lamb and slice. Serve topped with red wine gravy.

Char Grilled NY Strip Steaks with Wild Mushroom Ragout

3 T. Butter
1 T. Shallots-minced
1 T. Garlic-minced
4 C. Sliced wild mushrooms (such as portabello, oyster, shiitake or
  crimini)
2 T. Worcestershire sauce
¼ C. Burgundy
½ C. Veal stock (chicken stock may be substituted)
1 tsp. kosher salt
1 T. Fresh thyme leaves
Fresh ground pepper to taste
4- 12 oz Center cut NY strip steak
Salt & pepper

Heat large sauté pan and melt butter. Add shallots and garlic and sauté for 1 minute. Add mushrooms and sauté for 5 minutes. Add worcestershire, burgundy and veal stock. Simmer mushroom mixture for an additional 5 minutes until most liquid is absorbed. Season with salt, thyme and fresh ground pepper. Remove from heat.

Season steaks with salt and pepper. Grill steaks over medium high heat for 4 minutes on each side for medium rare. Top each steak with wild mushroom ragout.

Grilled Filet Mignon Gorgonzola

SERVES 4

4-8 oz. Center cut filet mignon
Salt and pepper
½ C. Dry white wine
2 tsp. Fresh garlic, minced
1 tsp. Shallots, minced
½ C. Sundried tomatoes, julienned
1 C. Gorgonzola, crumbled
1 T. Butter
3 C. Arugula-stems removed, washed & dried

Season steaks with salt & pepper on both sides. Grill over medium high heat for 4-5 minutes per side for medium rare. Heat a large sauté pan and add white wine, garlic, shallots and sundried tomatoes. Reduce mixture by half. Add gorgonzola, butter and arugula. Toss mixture quickly to melt butter and wilt arugula. Serve mixture atop filets.

I know this sounds like a crazy recipe. I developed this recipe for a contest.
A cattle association wanted recipes for an under-utilized cut of beef.
The marinade makes this incredibly tender and if you don't want to try
the coffee, omit it. It will still be a fantastic dish.

Molasses and Coffee Roasted Top Sirloin "Pastrami"

. . . .

SERVES 6

6 Top Sirloin steaks-about 6 ½ oz. each
½ C. Balsamic vinegar
½ C. Molasses
3 T. Fresh ground coffee
1 ½ C. Veal stock
2 T. Coriander seed-fresh ground
2 T. cumin seed-fresh ground
2 T. Cracked black peppercorns
¾ T. Kosher salt
      Garnish
18 Large shiitake mushroom caps
Olive oil for brushing
Salt & pepper to taste
½ C. Mango-fine diced
1 T. Chives-snipped

Place top sirloins in a large mixing bowl. Add vinegar, molasses and coffee. Mix well and marinate for 3 hours. Remove sirloins from bowl, reserving marinade. Strain marinade through a fine sieve and place in saucepan with veal stock. Place mixture over medium high heat and reduce to about 1 cup. Keep warm.

Grill sirloins over medium high heat for 2 ½ minutes on each side for medium rare. Remove from grill. In a mixing bowl toss coriander, cumin, pepper and salt. Sprinkle top sirloins with spice mixture and let stand for about 3 minutes

Meanwhile, brush shiitake mushrooms with olive oil. Season with salt and pepper. Grill over high heat for about 20 seconds on each side. Remove from grill and keep warm. Slice sirloins on the bias and against the grain. Garnish with grilled shiitake mushrooms and sprinkle with diced mangoes and chives. Great with garlic mashed potatoes.

Veal Medallions with Champagne Mustard Sauce

SERVES 2

6-2 to 2 ½ oz. Veal cutlets
Flour for dredging veal
2 T. Olive oil
2 tsp. Shallots-minced
1 C. Shiitake mushrooms-sliced
½ C. Champagne
¼ C. Heavy cream
2 T. Veal demiglace (optional)
1 T. Sundried tomatoes (chopped)
2 T. Dijon mustard
2 tsp. Fresh chives-snipped
Salt and pepper to taste

Heat olive oil in a large sauté pan. Dredge veal in seasoned flour. Sear veal in pan for 45 seconds on each side. Remove from pan and keep warm in a 200° oven. Add shallots and mushrooms and sauté for 2 minutes. Add champagne and heavy cream and reduce by half. Add demiglace, sundried tomatoes and mustard and reduce an additional 2-3 minutes. Stir in chives and season with salt and fresh ground black pepper. Add veal to pan and coat with sauce. Serve.

The veal chop in this dish is well complimented by the sweet, spicy glaze
of the honey, roasted chiles and fresh mangoes. Be sure the veal chops
are frenched (the bone will be clean of fat). I find that a good veal chop is
one of the harder cuts of meat to find in your local market.
This will work with pork chops also.

Pan Roasted Veal Chop with Chili Lime Honey Glaze and Mango Salsa

SERVES 4

2 C. Mango (diced)
¼ C. Green chile peppers (roasted, peeled, seeded and diced)
¼ C. Red pepper (roasted, peeled, seeded and diced)
1 T. Chopped cilantro
1 T. Finely diced red onion
1 C. Honey
¼ C. Fresh lime juice
1 T. Ancho chile powder
2 tsp. Cumin seed (fresh ground)
½ tsp. kosher salt
1 C. Dry white wine
4-12 oz. Veal rib chops (frenched)
3 T. Grapeseed oil

Mix mango, green chile, roasted red peppers, cilantro and red onion and refrigerate. Place honey, lime juice, ancho chile powder, cumin seed and kosher salt in a saucepan and simmer for 5 minutes. Remove from heat. Heat large sauté pan and add 2 teaspoons grapeseed oil. Sear veal chop for 1 minute on each side. Pour honey mixture over top of veal. Deglaze pan with white wine. Place veal chop in 400° oven and cook to desired doneness. The honey and wine mixture will become caramelized and give the veal chop a wonderful glaze. If you don't have a pan large enough, use two separate sauté pans.

When serving veal, drizzle remaining honey mixture over veal chops. Garnish with fresh mango salsa.

There is nothing terribly original about this recipe. However, I feel it is one of the classic dishes served all too infrequently these days.

Osso Bucca

. . . .

SERVES 4

* 8 ea. 10-12oz. Veal shanks-tied
Salt and pepper
Flour for dredging veal
6 T. Olive oil
2 C. Onions-diced
2 T. Garlic-minced
1 C. White wine
4 C. canned plum tomatoes-chopped
1 T. Fresh thyme
1 T. Fresh oregano
1 T. Fresh rosemary
2 ½ Qt. Veal stock
2 T. Basil
2 T. Capers
1 T. Lemon zest

Place a heavy-bottomed sauté pan over medium high heat. Add olive oil. Season veal with salt & pepper. Dredge in flour. Sauté veal for 3 minutes on each side until nicely browned. Place veal in a deep baking pan in a single layer.

Add onion and garlic to pan and cook for 3-4 minutes until lightly browned. Add white wine and cook additional 2 minutes. Add plum tomatoes, thyme, oregano, rosemary and veal stock. Bring mixture to a boil, then reduce to a simmer for 15 minutes. Pour over veal shanks. Cover and cook in a 350° oven for 2-2 ½ hours. Veal should be very tender to the touch. Remove from juices and keep warm. Reduce cooking liquids for 10 minutes. Remove string and top with tomato reduction. Sprinkle with basil, capers and lemon zest.

* Be sure to tie the outside of the veal shanks. This will help the veal keep it's shape during cooking.

Pastas, Grains, Potatoes
& Vegetables

Grains

. . . .

Arborio Rice

The word "risotto" makes many a home cook and chef uncomfortable. It was always an intimidating dish for me to make in a restaurant setting. I always remembered the classic Italian restaurants that said "allow 30 minutes for preparation." However, it is quite possible to prepare much of this fabled dish ahead of time. At Radnor Valley we prepare 15-20 orders of risotto ahead of time, stopping after the risotto has had the last addition of stock. We spread the risotto out flat on a sheet pan and cool it quickly. When it is time to serve, we finish the risotto according to the recipe that night. Doing this at home will save you a lot of time and worry when serving this special dish. *Hint-be sure to use a heavy bottomed pan.

Risotto is made from an Italian short grain rice, the most popular by far being arborio. Italian favorites include the fast cooking, but firm, *vialone nano*, and the rare *carnaroli*.

Quinoa (keen-wah)

Quinoa is a grain native to the South American Andes, but has recently been harvested in the United States and China. The high protein grain is also abundant with essential nutrients, such as calcium & phosphorous. Quinoa has a rich, nutty flavor worth trying and is a great substitute for rice or potatoes. Available in gourmet food stores.

Cous Cous

Cous cous is not a grain, as many think, but actually a pasta. Traditional preparation of this North African staple is very labor intensive. Semolina flour is sprinkled with salted water, then rubbed to separate the lumps. Then it is passed through a fine sieve to separate each granule. It is then steamed in a special pot called a couscoussiere. Fortunately, there is a quick cooking rendition of cous cous readily available in the market today. This is a great item to use when you don't have time to cook potatoes or rice. It lends itself to flavors very well.

Israeli Cous Cous

This is a much larger variation of cous cous. It is much more similar in taste and texture to a pasta. It takes about 10 minutes in boiling water and is also a nice change of pace as a starch. It also holds up quite well to cooking ahead of time and reheating when needed. I like to sauté the cooked product with olive oil, garlic and fresh spinach for a quick side dish.

Barley

Barley is a very underutilized grain. Pearl barley is by far the most common. Hulled barley, which holds many more nutrients, can be found in health food stores. However, realize that the cooking time for hulled barley is twice as long. Toasting the barley, as mentioned in this book (Pan Seared Duck Breast w/Toasted Barley Salad) is a great way of giving this grain added flavor.

Potatoes

Though there are many varieties, they are basically divided into two types-waxy and mealy. When choosing a potato be sure it is firm and heavy in the hand. There should be no green discoloration and sprouted eyes. *Waxy Types* Generally called an all purpose potato. These potatoes have a low starch content, but are high in moisture. This best suits them for boiling, as they will not fall apart easily. They are also very good for making potato salad and roasting. Red or new potatoes fall into this category. *Mealy Potatoes* Generally called a baker-such as an Idaho or Russet. These potatoes contain a high starch content that makes them wonderful for baked, mashed or using in a gratin.

Sweet Potatoes

Very often they are wrongly identified as yams. Sweet potatoes may be orange, white or yellow fleshed. A true yam, is at times, much larger than sweet potatoes. The color of the flesh varies and its flavor is not as sweet.

Be aware that a potato varies in flavor according to the time of the year and how it is stored. Starch content increases with maturity. Never refrigerate. Keep in a dark, cool place and do not expose to sunlight.

In reference to genetic engineering which is being used more often today. Potato farmers had been having trouble with whole crops being lost to sub-freezing weather. Scientists have introduced a gene from a species of flounder that lives in zero degree waters into certain strains of potatoes. These potatoes can now withstand temperatures up to 10 degrees below freezing. Interesting and eerie at the same time.

Vegetables

· ·

It was not many years ago that the seasons defined what vegetables and fruit were in the marketplace. But today with improved transportation, modernized cultivation practices and genetic engineering, there is a bounty of choices. However, I personally feel that too many people overlook fresh vegetables as a steady part of their diet. I did not spend too much time with vegetable recipes. When I cook at home I usually steam my vegetables and then drizzle with extra virgin olive oil, garlic, salt and pepper. I love the flavor of fresh beets simply roasted whole with olive oil, then peeled and seasoned with salt and pepper. I also love to cook greens- broccoli raab, mustard, collard and beet. Don't pass up the opportunity to easily prepare vegetables on your outdoor grill. Slice zucchini, yellow squash and onions (even carrots). Brush with olive oil, salt and pepper. Grill for 1-2 minutes on each side and serve.

Another time saver is blanching your vegetables ahead of time. For example, you can cook your fresh green beans or broccoli for 2 minutes in boiling water. Remove and place in an ice bath to stop the cooking process. You can then reheat your vegetables in a sauté pan with olive oil or butter and your favorite spices. Whatever method you use you should take advantage of the beautiful variety offered in today's supermarkets and produce outlets.

Heirloom Tomatoes

The advent of mega-agriculture in America has seen the gradual depletion of ancient varieties of native non-hybrid plants. Unfortunately, for those of us who appreciate full flavored tomatoes, we have seen a decline in quality and flavor. Commercial breeders focus only on strains that have mass-market appeal. They are mass-produced with thick skins that hold up to long distance shipping. They are picked somewhat green and have the ability to ripen after harvest. They are beautiful, symmetrical and hardy, but the flavor suffers.

However, some 25 years ago some dedicated individuals began saving open pollinated seed varieties, which have become known as Heirloom seeds. Often they are the product of generations of seed saving and selective breeding. They are flavorful, fragrant and are very nutritional. The public is becoming more aware of Heirloom vegetables and farmers are taking notice. You can find them at some local farm markets and specialty produce markets. For more information, search the World Wide Web under "Heirloom Vegetables." You will find companies that will sell you Heirloom vegetables, as well as seeds to grow your own. It is worth the effort! Enjoy.

This is a variation on basil pesto. Be sure not to overprocess the arugula when making the pesto. You want it to retain its bright, green color.

Grilled Chicken, Fettuccine & Arugula Pesto

. . . .

SERVES 4

4 C. Packed arugula, washed & dried
¼ C. Pine nuts, toasted
2 Garlic cloves
½ C. Parmesan cheese
⅓ C. Olive oil
4-4 oz. Boneless, skinless chicken breast
1 tsp. Garlic-minced
1 T. Balsamic vinegar
1 T. Olive oil
Salt & pepper to taste
1 Lb. Fettuccine
Reserved pasta water as needed

Place arugula, pine nuts, and garlic in bowl of food processor. Puree mixture until chopped fine. Add parmesan cheese. With machine running slowly add olive oil and process until smooth. Remove from bowl and season with salt & pepper.

Toss chicken breast with minced garlic, vinegar & oil. Let marinate up to 6 hours. Grill chicken over medium high heat for 3-4 minutes per side, depending on thickness of breast. Keep warm.

Cook fettuccine according to package directions, reserving about 1 cup of cooking liquid. Toss hot fettuccine with pesto, thinning with reserved pasta water to desired consistency. Julienne chicken breast and toss with fettuccine. Serve immediately.

Capellini with Gorgonzola and Tomatoes

SERVES 4

2 T. Olive oil
1 C. Onions-diced
3 T. Garlic-minced
½ C. Tomato puree
3 Lb. Ripe tomatoes-peeled, seeded & diced
8 oz. Gorgonzola-crumbled
3 T. Fresh basil-chopped
Oven dried tomatoes (see recipe) or
¼ C. Sundried tomatoes-softened in hot water for 1 minute
¼ C. Extra virgin olive oil
1 Lb. Capellini

In a small saucepan heat olive oil. Add onion and garlic and sauté for 4 minutes. Add tomato puree and simmer for 5 minutes.

Cook capellini according to package directions. Drain well and place in a large serving bowl. Toss pasta with tomato puree mixture, diced tomatoes, gorgonzola, basil, sundried tomatoes and extra virgin olive oil. Mix well and serve.

If you are like me and you end up with a large number of tomatoes from your garden, try this recipe.

Oven Dried Tomatoes

10 Ripe Plum Tomatoes
Olive oil for brushing
Kosher salt and fresh ground black pepper
1 ½ T. Fresh basil-chopped
2 tsp. Fresh garlic-minced
⅓ C. Extra virgin olive oil

Preheat oven to 150°. Cut tomatoes in half and remove core and seeds. Place tomatoes on a baking sheet, cut side up. Brush tomatoes with olive oil and sprinkle with kosher salt and black pepper. Bake in oven for 8-10 hours or until tomatoes are half their size, but still moist.

Remove tomatoes from tray and toss with basil, garlic and olive oil. Place in an airtight container and keep at room temperature for 3-5 days. They will keep longer in refrigerator, just bring to room temperature before serving. Wonderful in salads, pastas and with grilled chicken or fish.

The following three recipes are for when you need a quick, easy dinner. See what can be prepared ahead of time for even quicker dinner service.

Linguini with Broccoli Raab and Tomatoes

3 lbs. Broccoli raab, large stems removed, washed
3 T. Fresh garlic-minced
1 T. & ¼ C. Olive oil
½ C. White wine
1 C. Chicken stock
1 T. Cornstarch
2 T. Water
14.5 oz. Can diced tomatoes in juice
1 lb. Linguini
¾ C. Parmesan cheese
3 T. Fresh basil-chopped

Fill a large stockpot with water and bring to a boil. Add broccoli raab and blanch for 1 minute. Remove from water, drain and spread out on a baking sheet to cool. Can be prepared 1 day ahead.

Heat a medium saucepan and add 1 T. olive oil. Sauté 1 T. garlic for 2 minutes. Add white wine and chicken stock and bring to a boil. Reduce heat to a simmer and cook for 5 minutes. Mix cornstarch with water to form a paste. Stir into simmering stock to thicken. Add diced tomatoes and reduce heat to low.

In a large sauté pan heat ¼ cup olive oil. Add 2 T. garlic and sauté for 1 minute, stirring to keep garlic from browning. Add broccoli raab to pan, stir to coat with garlic and oil. Cover pan and cook over medium heat for 4-5 minutes. Cook linguini according to package directions. Drain pasta well. In a large serving bowl place half of tomato mixture and half of broccoli raab. Add pasta and top with remaining tomato mix and broccoli raab. Toss with parmesan and basil.

Penne Pasta with Roasted Garlic Walnut Sauce
SERVES 4

1 Large head garlic, brushed with olive oil
1 C. Walnuts
⅓ C. Olive oil
⅓ C. Chicken stock
1 tsp. Salt
Fresh ground black pepper
1 lb. Penne pasta
1 C. Gorgonzola, crumbled
2 T. Fresh basil, chopped

Wrap garlic in aluminum foil and roast in 400° oven for 45 minutes or until soft. When cool, cut off top and press out roasted garlic. Place in food processor and add walnuts. Process mixture while slowly adding olive oil and chicken stock. Remove from processor and season with salt & pepper.

Cook penne pasta according to package directions. Drain and place pasta in serving bowl. Toss sauce with hot pasta and coat well. Stir in gorgonzola and basil. Serve with french bread.

Mediterranean Pasta

3 T. Olive oil
1 C. Onions-diced
2 T. Garlic-minced
½ C. Dry white wine
4 C. Diced tomatoes in puree
3 T. Capers
3 T. Fresh basil-chopped
¼ C. Pitted calamata olives-chopped
Salt and pepper to taste
1 Lb. Penne, farfalle or rotini (cook to package directions)
¾ C. Crumbled feta cheese

Heat medium saucepan and add olive oil. Add onion and garlic and cook for 5 minutes, stirring occasionally until lightly browned. Deglaze pan with white wine. Simmer for 3 minutes. Add tomatoes and cook additional 5 minutes. Stir in capers, basil and olives. Season with salt and pepper.

Toss cooked pasta with tomato sauce. Garnish with crumbled feta cheese. This sauce is great with chicken, fish and pork.

This is a nice variation on fresh tomato sauce. I like to finish this sauce with a small amount of butter and serve over ravioli or pasta. Garnish with fresh grated parmesan and some crispy proscuitto.

Yellow Tomato Sauce

MAKES ABOUT 6 CUPS

6 Yellow beefsteak tomatoes
1 T. Extra virgin olive oil
3 T. Onion-finely diced
1 T. Roasted garlic
2 T. Fresh basil-chopped
White wine

Score bottom of tomato in an X pattern. Place in a pot of boiling water for 20 seconds. Remove and place in a bath of ice water for 15 seconds. Remove from water and peel off skin. Core tomatoes. Cut tomatoes in half and gently remove seeds. Dice tomatoes and set aside.

Heat a medium sauté pan. Add olive oil, onion and garlic. Cook for 2 minutes. Add white wine and cook additional minute. Add tomatoes and heat through. Place tomato mixture in food processor and process until smooth. Remove from bowl. Add basil and season with salt and pepper.

This dish is great hot or cold. If serving chilled, place on a bed of mixed baby greens lightly tossed with toasted sesame seed vinaigrette. Either way, it is complemented quite nicely by grilled shrimp, scallops or chicken.

Asian Noodles with Macadamia Nut Ginger Pesto

SERVES 4

½ C. Roasted macadamia nuts-chopped
2 Garlic cloves
2 T. Pickled ginger
1 ½ C. Coriander leaves-rinsed & dried
1 C. Flat leaf parsley-rinsed & dried
½ C. Fresh basil
⅓ C. olive oil
2 T. Sesame oil
* 1 T. Sriracha- asian hot sauce
1 Lb. Asian noodles or linguini
⅔ C. Reserved pasta cooking liquid

* Available in Asian markets

In a food processor blend macadamia nuts, garlic, ginger, coriander, parsley and basil until smooth. With processor on slowly add olive and sesame oils. Season with sriracha and salt to taste.

Cook pasta according to package directions. When draining reserve ⅔ cup cooking liquid. Drain pasta and toss with reserved cooking liquid and macadamia nut pesto.

Serve these rice dishes with your favorite Chicken, Fish or Meat Dishes

Toasted Coconut Rice

SERVES 4 - 6

1 T. Grapeseed oil
1 tsp. Fresh ginger, minced
2 T. Fresh, shredded coconut
¼ C. Unsalted peanuts, chopped
2 C. Chicken stock
1 C. Coconut milk
1 Lemongrass stem
1 tsp. Ground cumin seed
½ tsp. Ground cardamom
2 ½ C. Basmatic Rice

Heat oil in a 4 qt. Dutch oven. Add ginger, peanuts and coconut. Sauté for 2-3 minutes until coconut and peanuts are a golden brown. Add chicken stock, coconut milk and lemongrass stem. Bring mixture to a boil, then reduce heat to a simmer for 5 minutes. Add cumin and cardamom and return to a boil. Add basmati rice and cook uncovered until steam holes appear (about 12 minutes). Remove lemongrass stem and serve.

Green Chile Scented Rice

SERVES 4 - 6

2 T. Butter
1 T. Garlic-minced
½ C. Onion-diced
2 C. White rice
4 C. Chicken stock
1 tsp. Salt
2 T. Green onions-sliced thin
2 T. Cilantro-chopped
3 T. Diced green chilies (canned)
½ C. Diced tomatoes

In a medium saucepan melt butter over medium high heat. Sauté garlic and onion for 4 minutes until lightly browned. Stir in rice, chicken stock and salt. Cover and reduce heat to a simmer. Cook for about 15 minutes or until liquid is absorbed. Remove from heat. Stir in green onions, cilantro, green chilies and diced tomatoes.

If you want to make these pancakes ahead of time, here's a little tip. Boil your potatoes, depending on size, until they are halfway cooked. Let cool, then peel. You can now proceed from the beginning of the recipe. The cooking process will keep the potatoes from turning brown, allowing you to make the pancakes ahead of time.

Crispy Potato Pancakes

3 Large Idaho potatoes-peeled
2 T. Minced onion
2 Eggs, beaten
Salt and fresh ground black pepper
Fresh ground nutmeg (optional)
4 T. Clarified butter

Grate potatoes with a hand grater or a food processor attachment. Mix in onion, egg, salt, pepper and nutmeg. Heat a large sauté pan and add clarified butter. Spoon 3 tablespoons of mixture into pan, spreading out evenly to about ½ in. thick. Cook for about 2 minutes on each side. Remove from pan and place in a 375° oven for about 5 minutes to finish cooking process. If thinner pancakes are desired, spread batter to a ¼ in. thickness and sauté for 2 minutes per side. There is no need to finish these in the oven.

The variations of mashed potatoes today are unlimited. You can add caramelized onions, roasted peppers, gorgonzola, or whatever your imagination or taste buds conjure up. The main thing to remember, a food mill or ricer makes the best potatoes. However, you can make great potatoes with a mixer, just don't overmix.

Roasted Garlic Mashed Potatoes

1 Head garlic-brushed with olive oil
8 Idaho potatoes-about 4 lbs.
¾ C. Chicken stock
¼ C. Heavy cream
4 T. Unsalted butter
1 tsp. Salt
¼ tsp. White pepper
2 T. Fresh snipped chives

Wrap garlic in aluminum foil. Roast in a 400° oven for about 45 minutes or until soft. When cool, cut off very top of garlic. Squeeze out roasted garlic. Mash with a fork and reserve for later use.

Peel potatoes and cut in quarters. Place potatoes in a pot and cover completely with water. Simmer potatoes for about 25 minutes or until tender. Drain potatoes and force through a ricer or food mill into a mixing bowl. If a ricer or food mill is not available, begin mixing potatoes at this point. With potatoes in a mixing bowl, add roasted garlic, chicken stock, cream, butter, salt and pepper. With electric beaters whip potatoes until completely smooth. Stir in fresh chives.

You can make this dish up to 3 days ahead. Polenta is a great alternative to potatoes or rice. You could substitute parmesan for gorgonzola or add some sundried tomatoes or roasted peppers for a change of pace. Polenta may also be eaten as a thick, soft puree if you do not want to let it set to harden.

Grilled Gorgonzola and Basil Polenta

3 C. Chicken stock
4 C. Milk
1 T. Fresh garlic-minced
2 tsp. Salt
½ tsp. Black pepper
2 C. Coarse yellow cornmeal
1 C. Gorgonzola-crumbled
2 T. Fresh basil-chopped

Bring stock, milk, garlic, salt and pepper to a boil. Reduce to a simmer and slowly whisk in cornmeal. Whisk constantly to avoid any lumps. Keep at a simmer for 15-20 minutes, stirring occasionally. The polenta should be very thick and pull away from the sides of the pan when stirred. Remove from heat and stir in gorgonzola and basil.

Place polenta in a buttered loaf or baking pan to cool. Press polenta into all corners of pan to insure an even loaf without any air pockets. Cover loosely with plastic wrap and refrigerate 10 hours or overnight.

Remove polenta from pan and cut into ¾ in. thick slices. Brush with olive oil and grill over high heat for about 1 minute on each side, or until heated through. You could also sauté the polenta in a hot pan with butter or olive oil. Serve with marinara sauce or drizzled with extra virgin olive oil.

Asian Marinated Asparagus

1 Lb. Asparagus-trimmed
1 tsp. Fermented black beans-well rinsed and chopped finely
2 tsp. Soy sauce
¼ C. Red onion-thinly sliced
2 T. Rice wine vinegar
1 T. Grapeseed oil
1 tsp. Sesame oil
2 T. Cilantro-chopped
½ tsp. Salt
1 tsp. Sriracha-asian hot sauce

Bring two quarts of water to a boil. Blanch asparagus in boiling water for 2-3 minutes. Remove from water and refresh in an ice bath.

Drain asparagus and toss with fermented black beans, soy sauce, ginger, red onion, rice vinegar, grapeseed oil, sesame oil, cilantro, salt and sriracha. Toss well and let marinate in refrigerator for 1-2 hours. Serve chilled with grilled chicken, fish or steak.

Asparagus and Greek Olive Sauté
. . . .

2 T. Extra virgin olive oil
2 tsp. Garlic-minced
* ¾ C. Assorted Greek olives, pitted & halved
1 Lb. Pencil asparagus (stems removed)
¼ tsp. Salt
Fresh ground black pepper to taste
¼ C. Water
½ C. Crumbled feta

* *Such as calamata, Mt. Pelion or Mt. Athos*

    Place a large sauté pan over medium high heat and add olive oil. Add garlic and olives and sauté for 1-2 minutes. Add asparagus, salt, pepper and water. Reduce heat, cover and cook until asparagus is tender, about 4 minutes. Remove from heat, sprinkle with feta cheese and serve.

Mango Scented Quinoa

SERVES 4

2 T. Unsalted butter
¼ C. Onion-minced
2 tsp. Fresh garlic-minced
* 1 C. Quinoa
1 tsp. Ground coriander
1 tsp. Ground cumin seed
2 C. Chicken stock
½ C. Fresh mango puree
½ C. Fresh mango-diced
1 T. Fresh cilantro-chopped
¼ C. Red pepper-minced
Salt and fresh ground pepper to taste

See beginning of this chapter for description and information on this tasty grain

    Heat a medium saucepan and add butter. Add onion and garlic and sauté for 2-3 minutes. Add quinoa and sauté an additional 2 minutes. Add coriander, cumin and chicken stock. Bring to a boil, stir and then reduce heat to a simmer. Cover and cook for 15 minutes, stirring occasionally to prevent sticking. Remove from heat, stir in mango puree, diced mango, cilantro and red bell pepper. Season with salt and pepper and serve.

Here is a little used squash, mainly because people are unaware of how to cook it. It is a rather easy squash to prepare, as the following recipe shows.

Spaghetti Squash with Brandy Butter

SERVES 4

1 Large spaghetti squash
2 tsp. Olive oil
½ C. Brandy
4 T. Unsalted butter
1 T. Maple syrup

Cut squash in half and remove seeds. Brush outside of squash with olive oil. Place squash, cut side down on a baking pan and bake in a preheated 375° oven for about 1 hour, or until tender. Remove squash from oven and turn squash over. With a fork flake away the flesh into strands. Place squash in a serving bowl and keep warm. In a small saucepan place brandy over high heat until reduced by at least half. Stir in butter and maple syrup until fully incorporated. Drizzle brandy butter over spaghetti squash. Season with salt and fresh ground black pepper.

The following recipes are two easy alternatives to potatoes or rice. Each of them are served with duck, as examples, in the poultry chapter.

Toasted Barley Salad
. . . .

¾ C. Pearl barley
1 T. Butter
2 T. Onions-minced
1 T. Garlic-minced
½ C. Shiitake mushrooms-stemmed & diced
¼ C. White wine
2 C. Brown chicken stock
Salt & pepper to taste

Place barley in a heavy-bottomed saucepan. Add butter, onion, garlic, and shiitake mushrooms and place over medium heat. Stir mixture occasionally until barley is lightly toasted, about 10 minutes. Add white wine and chicken stock. Reduce heat to medium-low and simmer for about 30 minutes or until all stock is absorbed. Season with salt and pepper, and let cool. Serve at room temperature.

Ginger Scented Cous Cous
. . . .

1 T. Butter
1 tsp. Garlic-minced
¼ C. Onion-finely diced
8 oz. Israeli cous cous
2 ¼ C. Brown chicken stock
Salt and pepper to taste

In a 2 qt. saucepan heat olive oil. Sauté garlic and onion over medium heat for 2 minutes. Add cous cous and chicken stock. Bring to a boil. Turn heat to low and simmer until all liquid is absorbed, about 15 minutes. Season with salt and pepper.

Be sure to read the tips on cooking risotto mentioned at the beginning of this chapter. Risotto is well worth the extra time and before you know it you'll be a pro.

Wild Mushroom Risotto

4 C. Chicken stock
1 C. Veal stock
2 T. Worcestershire sauce
¼ C. Dried Porcinis
3 T. Butter
1 C. Onion-diced
1 T. Fresh garlic-minced
1 T. Shallots-minced
2 C. Shiitake mushrooms-stems removed and sliced
1 lb. Arborio rice
2 T. Fresh thyme leaves
3 T. Fresh grated parmesan cheese
Salt & pepper to taste
1 C. Heavy cream

Place veal stock, chicken stock, worcestershire and porcinis in 4 qt. stockpot and bring to a boil. Reduce heat to a simmer and cook for additional 45 minutes. Strain stock, reserving mushrooms. Puree mushrooms in food processor and reserve for later use.

In a heavy bottomed saucepan melt butter over medium high heat. Add onion, garlic, shallots and shiitake mushrooms. Sauté for 3 minutes, stirring occasionally. Add arborio rice and pureed porcinis and cook additional 2 minutes, stirring to keep rice from sticking. Deglaze pan with dry sherry. Add stock 1 cup at a time, stirring constantly to release starch from rice and keep from sticking. As stock is absorbed, add another cup until all stock is used. Remove from heat and add thyme, parmesan cheese and heavy cream. Serve immediately. If you like this dish lighter, the heavy cream can be omitted.

Heart Healthy

Your Guide to Good Fat-Yes, Good Fat

Very few groups have inspired as much controversy and confusion in recent years as the category of fats and oils. These products represent the most concentrated source of calories in the diet. Health experts recommend that fat intake be limited to no more than 30% of calories consumed. **See chart for fat formulas on next page.**

Fat can be reduced in your cooking, but I don't recommend trying to eliminate it entirely. Fats play a vital role in cooking-they lend flavor to food and contribute to a feeling of satiety (an important aspect if your dieting). Trim meats thoroughly or serve smaller portions instead of practicing no-fat cooking.

Not all fat is bad. Eating the right fats is essential to good health. As with everything in life, moderation and variety are the key. The following is a guide to help you make informative choices.

Good Fats

Olive Oil – Top favorite of health experts, it is highly monounsaturated. Monounsaturated is the safest fat of all. It tends to lower bad LDL cholesterol while preserving good HDL cholesterol.

Canola Oil – Excellent choice for a recipe that calls for cooking oil. High in monounsaturated, low in saturated fats. Rich in Omega 3 fatty acids. * (Omega 3 found in high-fat fish, i.e. Salmon)

Macadamia Nut Oil – Excellent-Highest of all salad oils in monounsaturated fats.

Grapeseed Oil – Good, high in antioxidants and has been shown to raise good HDL cholesterol.

Avocado Oil – OK. Like avocados, it is rich in monounsaturated fats.

Walnut Oil – OK. High in Omega 3's.

Flaxseed Oil – Used as a supplement by some health experts. Exceptionally rich in Omega-3's. Appears to have anti-cancer benefits. Sold in health food stores.

So-So Fats

Soybean Oil – OK sometimes. Best when eaten in Tofu and whole soybeans. Contains anti-oxidants that help neutralize the potentially detrimental effects of the oil itself. Bad side-Soybean oil is usually hydrogenated-making it harmful.

Peanut Oil – OK sometimes. High in bad Omega 6 fatty acids. (These promote cancer and immune malfunctions). Also contains relatively high amounts of monounsaturated. *Look for peanut butter without hydrogenated fats* *

Corn Oil – (Polyunsaturated Fat)-New studies say it is a risky choice. High in Omega 6 fatty acids. Saturated with oxygen, which release disease causing free radicals inside the body.

Safflower and Sunflower Oils – High in Omega 6 fatty acids. You do not have to eliminate these oils, just cut back.

Bad Fat

Trans-Fatty Acids – (Margarine) Trans fatty acids are created when vegetable oils are hardened, or hydrogenated. Some experts blame trans-fatty acids, especially margarine, for high rates of heart disease. Trans fats can be as bad as saturated fats in raising cholesterol. Restrict margarine and processed foods rich in hydrogenated/ partially hydrogenated oils. If you must, choose tub or liquid margarine over stick. Note: Packaged foods apt to be high in trans fat: Doughnuts, Crackers, French Fries, Microwave Popcorn, Peanut Butter, Cookies. Read labels!!!

Animal Fats – (Butter, Cheese, Meat Fat) Saturated fat is a prime enemy in raising cholesterol and clogging arteries.

Tropical Fats – (Palm & Coconut Oils) No reason to consume these vegetable fats which are 50-85 % saturated fat.

Fat Tips

- "Reduced Fat" on a food label means at least 25% less fat than usually found in that food.
- "Light" means half the fat, or one-third the calories.
- "Low Fat" means less fat, without quantifying it.
- "Olestra" new fake fat on the market used in chips and crackers. Reduces fat and calories, but also reduces antioxidants in the body. My opinion, wait a while before getting excited about it.
- Restrict saturated, polyunsaturated vegetable and hydrogenated fats.
- Read food labels and remember to keep your fat intake to 30 % of calories consumed.
- There are a lot of new flavored oil sprays to enhance low fat food.
- Beware, fat free desserts are still very high in calories and sugar.

Fat Formulas

1 gram of fat has 9 calories. 1 gram of protein or carbohydrate has only 4. 1 tablespoon of fat = about 14 g, = about 125 calories.

To figure haw much fat is in a particular food: If a serving of corn chips has 150 calories and 6 grams of fat, 6 g x 9 = 54 calories from fat. Divide 54 by 150 = 36 % calories derived from fat.

When you reduce fat in cooking, it helps to add spices, herbs, vinegars or wine to compensate for the loss of flavor. There are a lot of ways to make good low-fat food. Hopefully, I will help you accomplish this. There are a number of fat free dressings and snacks that will allow you to increase the fat consumption in your main meal or dessert. Enjoy!!

Here are 3 very simple, but very tasty snacks to try. Try them with the Creamy Roasted Garlic Dip, or one of the following salad dressings.

Crunchy Bread Snacks

Crispy Garlic Toast Rounds

Slice French bread into ¼ in.- ½ in. thick rounds. Lay rounds on baking sheet and lightly brush with olive oil or spray with a flavored cooking spray. Bake in 350° oven until brown (about 10 minutes). Remove and rub with fresh cut garlic. Try it with Salsa.

Fresh Baked Tortilla Chips

Lightly brush flour tortillas or spray with cooking spray. Sprinkle with chili powder, ground cumin and ground coriander. Cut each tortilla into 8 wedges. Spray baking sheet and lay wedges on pan. Bake at 350° for 6-8 minutes. Watch out, they burn soon after.

Fat Free Pita Chips

4 Pita pockets-separated into 2 sides
2 Egg whites-lightly beaten
1 tsp. Ancho chili powder
1 tsp. Kosher salt
1 tsp. Ground cumin

After separating pita, cut each into 8 wedges. Brush smooth side of pita with egg whites. Sprinkle wedges evenly with chili powder, salt and cumin. Bake at 350° for 10 minutes or until crisp. Be careful not to burn.

Creamy Roasted Garlic Dip

1 tsp. & 2 T. Canola oil
2 Heads garlic
3 T. Cider vinegar
2 T. Fresh tarragon (chopped)
½ tsp. Fresh ground black pepper
2 C. Plain non-fat yogurt

Brush garlic head with 1 tsp. canola oil. Wrap in foil and bake in 400° oven for 45 minutes or until soft. Let cool, cut off very top of garlic and squeeze out roasted garlic. Place garlic, vinegar, tarragon & pepper in food processor. Process for 5 seconds, scraping down sides once during this time. Add yogurt and process for 20 seconds until creamy. With processor on add remaining 2 T. canola oil and process for 15 seconds. Refrigerate for up to 1 week. Great with fat free pita chips.

Try this dressing on grilled fish, chicken or seafood. You need very little, as the arugula imparts a very intense flavor.

Fat Free Arugula Vinaigrette

2 C. Arugula, washed, dried-stems removed
2 T. Red onion-minced
½ C. Fresh squeezed orange juice
½ C. Mango or cantaloupe-diced
¼ C. Honey
1 T. Fresh lime juice
1 T. Raspberry vinegar
Salt to taste

Place all ingredients in blender and mix on high. You may have to turn blender off once or twice to incorporate arugula. Continue to blend until mixture is smooth. You want to have a bright, fresh, green color to your vinaigrette.

Salad Dressings

Creamy Cottage Cheese Dressing – Makes about 1 ½ cups. This is a good base for a number of dressings that are extremely low in fat.

1 C. Low fat cottage cheese
⅓ C. Low fat buttermilk
1 T. Balsamic vinegar

Place ingredients in a blender or food processor and mix until very smooth. If thinner consistency wanted, add more buttermilk.

Blue Cheese Dressing

Add 2 T. crumbled Gorgonzola or Roguefort cheese, cracked black pepper, fresh chives.

French Dressing

Add 2 tsp. ketchup, ½ tsp. paprika, 2 tsp. worcestershire, 1 tsp. tomato juice, ½ tsp. minced garlic, 2 tsp. dijon mustard, black pepper to taste.

Creamy Italian

Add 1 T. fresh basil, 1 tsp. fresh oregano, 1 tsp. fresh minced garlic, 2 tsp. fresh parsley, 2 T. balsamic vinegar, black pepper to taste.

Thousand Island

Add 2 T. pickle relish, 2 T. chili sauce, 2 tsp. dijon mustard.

Caesar

Add 3 minced anchovies, 1 T. minced garlic, 2 tsp. lemon juice, 2 T. parmesan cheese, 1 T. minced capers, 2 tsp. dijon mustard.

Radnor Valley Low Fat Crabcake

MAKES 12 CRABCAKES

(Per serving-about 3-1/2 grams of fat, 160 calories, 20% calories from fat)

2 lbs. Jumbo lump crabmeat
3 T. Minced onion
3 T. Minced red pepper
2 tsp. Canola oil
3 T. White wine
1 T. Fresh chopped parsley
2 T. Fresh lemon juice
½ C. Panko Breadcrumbs, + ½ cup breadcrumbs
2 Lg. Eggs
4 T. Non fat sour cream
3 T. Milk
1 ½ T. Dijon mustard
2 ½ tsp. Old Bay
¼ tsp. Fresh ground black pepper
Dash of tabasco sauce

Heat canola oil in small sauté pan. Add onion and peppers, and cook for 2 minutes, stirring occasionally. Add white wine and cook over high heat for 1 minute. Add mixture to jumbo lump crabmeat in a large mixing bowl. Toss in parsley, lemon juice and ½ cup of breadcrumbs. *Always gently toss crabmeat when mixing with other ingredients so that the crabmeat holds its shape.*

In a separate bowl, mix eggs, sour cream, milk, mustard, Old Bay, black pepper and tabasco. Mix thoroughly. Toss this with the crabmeat mixture. If too wet, add a little more breadcrumbs. Loosely form 12 crabcakes. Not packing the crabcake tight will give it a light, creamy texture. Sprinkle the crabcakes with the remaining panko breadcrumbs.

Spray a cookie sheet with non-stick cooking spray and place crabcakes on sheet. Bake in a preheated 400° oven for 10-15 minutes. You can finish under a broiler to give the crabcakes more color.

Note: You could sauté these in a small amount of canola oil for added flavor and finish in the oven the same as above. The crabcakes would still be considered low fat.

*Here I go again! Tuna and mangoes! This is an easy, but very tasty dish.
The coolness of the mangoes & crème fraiche nicely compliment the
fiery peppercorns. This goes great with the mango scented quinoa
(see recipe in pasta/grain chapter).*

Pepper Seared Tuna Steaks with Mango Puree and Ginger "Créme Fraiche"

SERVES 4

4 each-8 oz. Tuna steaks (about 1 inch thick)
3 T. Green peppercorns
3 T. Pink peppercorns
2 T. Black peppercorns
2 T. Grapeseed oil
1 C. Fresh mango puree

Using a mortar and pestle grind the three peppercorns with the grapeseed oil to form a paste. Spread the peppercorn mixture evenly on the tuna steaks and let marinate.

Heat a dry cast iron skillet until it is very hot. Sear tuna steaks for about 1 ½ minutes on each side for medium rare. Be careful, the tuna will continue to cook when removed from the pan. Garnish each steak with the mango puree and ginger créme fraiche.

Ginger Créme Fraiche

½ C. Nonfat sour cream
1 T. Buttermilk
1 T. Pickled ginger
Salt & pepper to taste
1 tsp. Rice wine vinegar

Place all ingredients in food processor and blend until smooth. I like to put sauce in a squirt bottle. This allows you to decorate the plate with the sauce.

If red snapper is not available, try flounder, striped bass or halibut. Try the smoked tomato salsa on grilled chicken and steaks, too.

Steamed Red Snapper, Smoked Tomato Avocado Salsa

. . . .

SERVES 4

4- 6 oz. Red snapper fillets
2 tsp. Olive oil
4 tsp. White wine
4 pieces Parchment paper

Brush each fillet with olive oil and sprinkle with white wine. Wrap each fillet in parchment. Bake in a 400° oven on a baking pan sprayed with non-stick cooking spray. Roast, seam side down for 8-10 minutes. Garnish with smoked tomato salsa.

Smoked Tomato Salsa

. . . .

2 Ripe, medium tomatoes
4 T. Avocado, diced
2 T. Yellow pepper, minced
2 T. Red onion, minced
2 T. Green onion, chopped
2 T. Fresh lime juice
1 T. Capers
1 tsp. Ground cumin
¼ tsp. Ground black pepper
2 T. Fresh cilantro-chopped
1 C. Mesquite wood chips-soaked for 15 minutes
Stovetop smoker

Place soaked wood chips in bottom of smoker and place over medium heat. Place grate in bottom of smoker and set tomatoes on top. Cover and let wood chips begin to smoke. Remove from heat and let tomatoes sit, covered, for 20-30 minutes. This will give the tomatoes a nice smoky flavor.

Remove tomatoes, core, seed and dice. Toss tomatoes with remaining ingredients. Serve atop steamed fish.

Honey Mustard Glazed Atlantic Salmon

SERVES 4

2 tsp. Olive oil
4-6oz. Atlantic salmon fillets-skinless, bones removed
2 tsp. Shallots-minced
¼ C. Dry white wine
¼ C. Dijon mustard
¼ C Honey
1 T. Fresh tarragon-chopped

Place a large sauté pan over high heat and add olive oil. Place salmon, skinned side up, and cook for 3-4 minutes. Turn salmon and carefully drain off excess fat. Add shallots and white wine and reduce for 1-2 minutes. Add mustard, honey and tarragon. Mix well and baste salmon with sauce. Place salmon under a preheated broiler for 2 minutes to finish. This will give the salmon a nice glaze.

Roasted Red Pepper & Tomato Coulis

2 T. Extra virgin olive oil
2 tsp. Fresh garlic, minced
1 tsp. Shallots-minced
1 tsp. Jalapeno peppers-minced
1 C. Plum tomatoes-skinned, seeded & diced
1 C. Roasted red peppers
1 C. Chicken stock
¼ Balsamic vinegar
Salt and fresh ground black pepper to taste

Place a medium saucepan over high heat. Add olive oil and sauté garlic, shallots, and jalapeno peppers for 1 minute. Add tomatoes, roasted peppers and chicken stock and reduce to a simmer for 5 minutes. Remove from heat and place mixture in a food processor with balsamic vinegar. Puree until smooth and season with salt & pepper.

Serve over grilled fish, chicken or pasta. To enrich the sauce reheat in saucepan and add 3 T. butter and stir until melted.

Desserts

Bread pudding is another dish that can have many variations. The following are two of my favorites. You can use any old danish, bread or even croissants. Just remember the better tasting the bread, the better tasting the pudding.

Pumpkin Bread Pudding

6 SERVINGS

5 C. Challah bread (cut into ¾ inch cubes)
4 large eggs
½ C. Milk
1 ½ C. Heavy cream
1 C. canned pumpkin
½ C. Brown sugar
1 tsp. Nutmeg
¼ t. Allspice
1 tsp. Cinnamon
2 tsp. Vanilla extract

Mix eggs, milk, heavy cream and pumpkin thoroughly. Stir in nutmeg, allspice, cinnamon, and vanilla. Toss bread with custard and let sit for about 20 minutes. Butter an 8 x 8 x 2 inch baking pan. Place bread pudding in pan and bake covered at 350° for 20 minutes. Remove foil cover and bake additional 15 minutes or until toothpick stuck in center of pudding is relatively dry. Serve warm with your favorite ice cream.

Chocolate Bread Pudding with Cinnamon Schnapps Cream

SERVES 6

5 C. Challah bread or croissants (cut into ¾ inch cubes)
½ C. Unsalted butter
½ C. Semi-sweet chocolate (cut into small pieces)
3 Large eggs
2 ½ C. Heavy cream
½ C. Confectioners sugar

In a double boiler, melt butter and chocolate until smooth. In a separate bowl, combine eggs, heavy cream and sugar. Mix thoroughly. Stir chocolate into egg custard. Pour chocolate custard over challah bread. Let stand for about 20 minutes.

Butter an 8 x 8 x 2 baking pan. Place bread pudding in pan and bake covered for 20 minutes. Remove cover and bake an additional 15 minutes or until center still trembles slightly. Serve warm with cinnamon schnapps cream.

Cinnamon Schnapps Cream

2 C. Heavy cream
½ C. Cinnamon Schnapps
1 Vanilla bean (halved lengthwise)
1 tsp. Ground cinnamon

In a heavy bottomed saucepan place heavy cream, schnapps, vanilla bean and cinnamon. Reduce mixture over medium high heat to ¾ C. Strain through a fine sieve and serve with chocolate bread pudding.

The first time I served this was at one of our many wine tastings. The first reaction was that it was a little unusual. But it is just an upbeat version of Mom's rice pudding. After tasting, I think everyone agreed.

Caramelized Peach Risotto Napoleon

SERVES 8

¼ Lb. Unsalted butter
1 T. Ginger-minced
1 Lb. Arborio rice
¼ C. Dark rum
3 C. Peach or apricot nectar
2 C. Fresh peach puree
1 C. Heavy cream
2 C. Fresh peaches-peeled & finely diced
6 Spring roll skins-cut into 4 triangles each
1 C. Fresh papaya puree-placed in squirt bottle
Fresh raspberries for garnish

In a heavy bottomed saucepan melt butter over medium high heat. Add ginger and arborio rice and sauté for 3 minutes, stirring occasionally to keep rice from sticking. Deglaze pan with dark rum. Add peach nectar 1 cup at a time, stirring constantly to release starch from rice. As liquid is absorbed, add another cup until all peach nectar is used. Add fresh peach puree and heavy cream and cook additional 3-4 minutes. Remove from heat and let stand 5 minutes. Place risotto in refrigerator and let chill.

Deep fry spring roll skins in a 350° oil until crisp and evenly browned. Remove from oil and place on paper towels to dry. Sprinkle with confectioner's sugar.

To assemble-with a small ice cream server (2 oz.) make 24 even scoops of risotto. For each serving starting with risotto make 3 alternate layers of rice and spring roll crisps. Sprinkle each serving with ¼ cup diced peaches, papaya puree and raspberries.

This recipe is for those of you, me included, that don't have an ice cream maker at home. This process does work, it just can't be done too far ahead of time.

Quick Mango Sorbet

· · · · · · · · · · · · · · · · · ·

SERVES 4

4 C. Fresh mango-diced
⅓ C. Fresh squeezed orange juice
¼ C. Sugar

Place fruit in a single layer on a baking sheet. Place in freezer until frozen solid.

Place frozen mango and orange juice in food processor. Blend until smooth, scraping down on sides, if needed. Add sugar and process for 2-3 seconds. Remove from processor and freeze.

Sorbet can be made up to 1 hour in advance. After 1 hour, sorbet begins to get icy. Serve garnished with fresh mint sprig.

* *Works well with fresh peaches or strawberries, too.*

This is an easy, but very tasty finish to any dinner party. I also love to serve this on top of bread pudding. Now that is probably my favorite of desserts.

Vanilla Ice Cream with Banana Bourbon Sauce

SERVES 8

1 C. Brown sugar
1 C. Butter-cut into cubes
⅓ C. Bourbon
1 tsp. Vanilla extract
3 C. Sliced banana
12 C. Premium vanilla ice cream

Place sugar, butter, bourbon and vanilla extract in top of a double boiler and place over simmering water. Slowly heat until mixture is smooth. Add bananas and heat through. Serve warm over vanilla ice cream.

*I came up with this dessert for two of our members (you know who you are)
who are celiac-they cannot tolerate gluten in their diet. It turned out to
be one of the most sinful of desserts. These individual chocolate cakes are a
stunning, yet simple ending to a dinner party.*

Flourless Chocolate Lava Cake

½ Lb. Bittersweet chocolate-chopped
½ Lb. Unsalted butter-cubed
4 Eggs
6 Egg yolks
5 T. Sugar
½ C. and 2 T. Fine Cornmeal

Brush six -4 oz. Ramekins with butter and set aside. Place chocolate and butter
on top of a double boiler. Slowly melt until mixture is slightly warmed (about 110°
on a candy thermometer).

In a mixer beat eggs, yolks and sugar until light and fluffy. Remove chocolate
from heat. Fold eggs into chocolate mixture. Stir in cornmeal. Divide chocolate
mixture among the ramekins and bake in a preheated 375° oven for about 6
minutes. The cakes will puff up and will pull slightly away from the sides (careful
when checking, the inside will be liquid). Remove from oven and carefully unmold
onto individual dessert plates. Garnish with fresh berries and a puree of fresh
mango.

Clementines

. . . .

Every year I look forward to November. That is the beginning of clementine season – which generally runs from November - February. Clementines, a member of the mandarin orange family, are becoming increasingly popular. They are very easy to eat, have very few seeds, if any, and are wonderfully sweet. They hail mainly from Spain because of the countries ideal climate. U.S. farmers continue to try to successfully harvest this gem of a fruit. Anyway, this is a recipe I came up with using clementines, though tangerines or any sweet orange can be substituted.

Clementine Créme Brulée

. . . .

4 Large eggs
1 Egg white
½ C. Heavy cream
1 ½ C. Clementine juice (about 16 clementines)
⅓ C. Granulated sugar
1 tsp. Fresh lemon juice
* 2 T. Turbinado sugar

In a bowl combine eggs, egg white and heavy cream and mix well. Add clementine juice, granulated sugar and lemon juice. Stir until sugar is dissolved.

Divide custard between four-6 oz. Ramekins. Place ramekins in a baking pan and pour in enough hot water to cover halfway up sides of ramekins. Cover pan with foil and bake for 25 minutes in a preheated 350° oven. Custards should be set but still trembling slightly. Remove ramekins from pan and chill, covered loosely with plastic wrap, for at least 3 hours and up to 2 days.

When ready to serve, top each custard with 2 tsp. of turbinado sugar. Place custards about 3 inches under a preheated broiler. This will caramelize the sugar and give you a crisp, crunchy top to this wonderful dessert. An alternative to using the broiler is a blowtorch, which many kitchens do.

* I recommend using turbinado sugar (sugar in the raw or purified raw sugar) opposed to granulated sugar. The raw sugar will give you a much nicer, evenly caramelized top to your créme brulée.

Glossary

Glossary

. . . .

Acidulated Water – a combination of a small amount of lemon juice and water. Prevents discoloration of certain fruits and vegetables (such as apples and artichokes.

Al Dente – term meaning "to the bite." Basically used to describe doneness of pasta or vegetables. Actually a sensory evaluation of when food is done cooking. Pasta should be firm, but without a hard center.

Ancho Chile Pepper – this is a dried Poblano pepper. The flavor ranges from mild to spicy. Roast dried peppers for 5 minutes in a 375° oven, then grind in spice mill for fresh chile powder.

Arrowroot – similar in make-up to cornstarch and can be used as a substitute. Does not impart chalky flavor when undercooked, like cornstarch.

Beurre Blanc – an emulsified sauce of shallots, wine and butter. The variations in flavorings of this sauce are endless. Can be a tricky sauce to make at first. Just be sure your pan is not too hot after reducing the wine and that your butter is chilled.

Blanch – cooking foods in boiling water for a short amount of time, then placing into an ice bath to stop cooking process. Helps reduce vegetables final cooking time, such as broccoli or green beans.

Blue Point Oysters – originally named for Blue Point, Long Island, the place where these oysters were originally harvested. The term is now used to describe many Atlantic oysters ranging in sizes of 2-4 inches. Prized for serving on the half shell.

Braise – the method of browning an item in small amount of fat and then cooking in liquid for a long period of time. The cooking process helps tenderize lesser cuts of meat (i.e. Brisket of Beef).

Brochette – wooden skewers of meat, chicken, seafood or vegetables. The French word for skewer.

Bruschetta – grilled slices of bread brushed with olive oil, garlic and herbs. There are many variations to this dish.

Caper – pickled bud of the caper bush that is native to the Mediterranean and Asia. Wonderful in salad dressings and served with smoked fish.

Caviar – the lightly salted eggs of the Sturgeon. Grading is determined by the size and color of the roe (eggs) and the species of Sturgeon. Beluga, the most expensive and considered the finest, are large, soft gray colored eggs. Next in line is Osetra, a light medium brown egg that is smaller than Beluga. Sevruga is the smallest and firmest in texture, with a grayish color. Malossol is a term used that describes the amount of salt used in the initial curing process. Roe from other fish such as salmon, whitefish and lumpfish is not considered caviar, no matter what the label reads. Caviar is wonderful served with buckwheat blinis and iced vodka.

Challah – light, Jewish yeast bread that is enriched with eggs. The best bread for bread pudding.

Chevre – French word for goat, used to refer to cheese made with goat's milk. It's unique flavor easily sets it apart from other cheeses. Most people either love this cheese or dislike it.

Chiffonade – a very fine julienne or shred of fresh herbs or lettuce.

Chine – refers to the backbone of an animal. Must be removed from the ribs of a rack of lamb. This allows you to cut between each lamb chop.

Coconut Milk – not the liquid found in the center of a coconut. This thick liquid is derived by steeping fresh coconut in hot water.

Coriander – the leaves of this plant, native to the Orient and Mediterranean, are known as Cilantro. Cilantro is definitely an acquired taste. The dried, ripe fruit of this plant are known as coriander seeds. These seeds are very fragrant and flavorful. The two items hold no resemblance to each other, though they are from the same plant.

Coulis – a puree of fresh fruits or cooked vegetables.

Créme Brulée – the French term for "burned cream."

Créme Fraiche – naturally thickened cream that has a sharp, tangy flavor. If not available, you can make it yourself. Mix heavy cream with buttermilk in an 8 to 1 ratio. Let stand, covered, in warm place until thickened – about 12-20 hours.

Crostini – toasted bread slices brushed with olive oil and finished with a variety of toppings.

Cumin – this ancient spice dates back to the Old Testament. The seed is the dried fruit of a plant in the parsley family. It is my favorite dried spice and is used extensively in Southwestern cuisine.

Deglaze – adding liquid such as wine, vinegar or stock to a hot pan after sautéeing and removing excess fats. It helps collect the scraps of food that stick to the pan during sautéeing or roasting foods. This process adds a huge amount of flavor to a dish.

Emulsify – mixing one liquid with another. Emulsion is accomplished by slowly adding one ingredient to another, while mixing rapidly. Classic examples of emulsion are mayonnaise and certain salad dressings.

Fennel – this is a widely misunderstood vegetable. Many think it imparts a flavor of licorice because it is often labeled as anise. Fennel is much sweeter and when cooked imparts an ever lighter flavor than when it is raw.

Fermented Black Beans – this Chinese specialty is actually small soybeans that have been preserved in salt. They are rather salty and pungent. They should be rinsed well and finely chopped before adding to sauces. Refrigerated they have a shelf life of up to 1 year. This is a fantastic addition to many dishes.

Foie Gras – The term in French means "goose liver," but it refers to the fattened liver of duck and geese. These livers are treasured for their rich, buttery texture. Primarily imported from French and Canada, the product must be received in the cooked state. However, there are breeders in the United States who sell fresh Foie Gras.

Gluten – the protein found in Wheat flours.

Grapeseed Oil – The oil extracted from Grapeseeds. It has a rather mild flavor and is great for flavored oils, salad dressings and for sautéeing (it has a high smoke point).

Guava – the main variety of this fruit is native to Florida, Hawaii, California and South America. The color of the skin can range from yellow to purple. The flesh goes from yellow to red. It is also available as a puree, juice, preserves and canned whole.

Hydrogenated Oil – the process of hardening unsaturated oil by heating into a semi-solid. This heating transforms it into a saturated fat. It has been proven that hydrogenated oils are worse than natural saturated fats. The hydrogenation process gives the oil a longer shelf life. However, it is at the expense of the consumer. This widely ignored fat is the root of many problems related to high cholesterol, blood pressure and obesity. Most products on supermarket shelves contain this fat but by reading labels you can find many very good alternatives.

Infusion – flavor extracted from an ingredient (i.e. garlic, herbs) by steeping them in a liquid such as stock, oil or vinegar.

Julienne – food, usually vegetables, cut into long, thin uniform strips.

Leek – related to garlic and onions it resembles a large scallion, but has a mild flavor. Choose leeks with crisp, bright green leaves and a clean looking white portion. The smaller the leek, the more tender it will be. Be sure to rinse after cutting to remove all dirt between layers.

Lemongrass – essential to Thai cuisine. This scallion looking herb has grayish green leaves and a sour lemon flavor. It is available in oriental markets (and some supermarkets), fresh or dried. It is a very good addition to marinades, but especially soups or stocks.

Magret – breast meat from a Mallard Duck, which are specially raised for Foie Gras. Breast are much larger and have a thinner layer of fat than a Long Island or Pekin Duck.

Marbling – thin streaks and flecks of fat that run throughout meat. It enhances flavor, juiciness and tenderness.

Mignonette – term used to describe finely chopped herbs, vegetables or peppercorns.

Mussels – there are dozens of species but the most abundant and best tasting is the Blue Mussel. Be sure when purchasing mussels that their shells are closed tightly or close quickly when tapped. This will ensure that the mussels are fresh.

Panko – breadcrumbs that have a coarse texture. Referred to as Japanese breadcrumbs.

Papaya – the Solo is the variety most often found in the United States. Grown in Hawaii and Florida it has a golden skin when ripe. The flesh is bright orange to yellow. The black peppery seeds are generally discarded, unless you are making a salad dressing. Choose fruit that is heavy in the hand and firm. When using as a sauce or marinade you can puree the flesh and seeds and strain through a fine sieve. The Papaya will ripen quickly in a paper bag at room temperature.

Passion Fruit – grown throughout the world this small, egg shaped fruit has a purple skin. The yellow flesh has a very tart but sweet flavor. Choose fruit that is heavy in the hand and firm. The black seeds can also be used. You can puree the flesh along with the seeds and then strain through a fine sieve. Supermarkets also carry canned nectar and sometimes frozen concentrate. This fruit is great for making ice cream, dessert sauces and marinades.

Poblano Pepper – dark green, almost black chile pepper. The darker the flesh the richer the flavor. It is grown in Mexico and the Southwestern United States. In its dried state it is known as an Ancho chile.

Prawn – this tends to be a rather confusing term. Loosely defined it is any shrimp that yields less than 10 to a pound. It also refers to a species of the lobster family that includes Langoustinos. They resemble tiny lobsters that run 6-8" long. Also refers to fresh water prawns (Mediterranean Blue Shrimp) which looks like a cross between a lobster and a shrimp.

Ramekin – a small baking dish that looks like a mini souffle dish. Used to make custards such as Créme Caramel and Créme Brulée.

Sashimi – a Japanese dish of raw fish or shellfish. Generally served with soy sauce, wasabi and pickled ginger. Only the freshest fish should be used for sashimi.

Smoke Point – state where an oil begins to emit smoke when heated. The higher the smoke point, the better the oil is for sautéeing or deep frying.

Spaghetti Squash – available year round, the flesh of this squash when cooked, separates into strands similar in appearance to spaghetti. When buying look for an even yellow color with a smooth skin and hard to the touch.

Tahini – a paste of pureed sesame seeds.

Tartare – used to describe the preparation of finely chopped raw beef or fish. (Salmon & Greek Olive Tartare)

Truffle – a very flavorful and aromatic tuber. Due to its scarcity and short growing season, this item can draw a very high price – up to $700.00 per lb. The full flavors of black truffles are achieved when cooked. The highly prized white truffles of Piedmont are best when shaved or grated directly on the dish right before serving.

Wasabi – Japanese horseradish. Available in a paste or powder. The powder is mixed with water to form a paste. Served with sushi and sashimi. Very potent.

Zest – outermost layer of the skin of citrus. Be sure to remove only outer skin (not the bitter white pith). Use a citrus zester or vegetable peeler. The flavor rich zest is great for desserts, marinades, vinaigrettes and sauces.

Gourmet Food Sources

. . . .

American Spoon Foods
Petroskey, Michigan
1-800-222-5886

Chef Larry Forgione has a mail order company that offers specialty barbeque sauces, dried wild mushrooms and berries, homemade jams and more.

Assouline and Ting
Philadelphia, Pennsylvania
1-800-521-4491

Visit any of their 3 locations. Wonderful source for chocolates, flavored oils, vinegars, caviar, foie gras, truffles, fleur de sel and cheeses.

Aux Petits Delices
Wayne, Pennsylvania
1-610-971-0300

Owner Patrick Gauthron offers fantastic chocolates, perfect croissants and first class desserts.

Balducci's
New York, New York
1-800-BALDUCCI

This famous New York market has a mail division. You can get prime meat, fresh and dried chiles and a wide array of specialty food products.

D' Artagnan
Jersey City, New Jersey
1-800-327-8246

You can mail order foie gras, free range chickens and assorted game.

Dean and DeLuca
New York, New York
1-800-221-7714

Great selection of cheeses, coffee, pasta and grains, aged balsamic vinegar and many more gourmet provisions. Try the Chocolate Babka. Mail order or visit one of their many locations.

Francescas Favorites
Hollywood, Florida
1-800-865-CRAB

Mail order Florida Stone Crab Claws, Spiny Lobsters and Key West Shrimp.

Le Bus Breads
Manayunk, Pennsylvania
1-215-930-0255

Wide range of specialty breads including raisin-pecan and black olive-cilantro sourdough.

Zagaras Specialty and Natural Foods
Mt. Laurel and Marlton, NJ
Jenkintown, PA

Visit any location for a great selection of organic produce, international cheeses, all natural meats and poultry, fresh exotic seafood, house roasted coffee and artisanal breads.

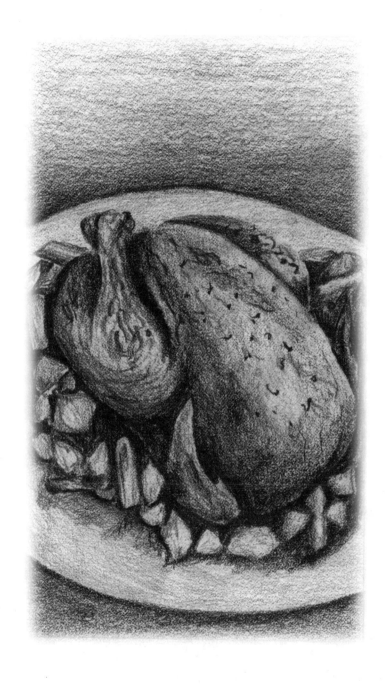

Index

Index

· · · · · · · · · · · · · · · · ·

Ordering Additional Copies

To order additional copies of this book please send your name, address and $17.00 per book plus $2.00 for shipping and handling to:

Private Cuisine
Greenleaf Enterprises
PO Box 291
Chesterland, OH   44026

You may also order with a credit card by calling (800) 932-5420 or visiting our site on the internet at www.greenleafenterprises.com. Remember that all the profits from the sale of this book go directly to the Make-A-Wish Foundation.

Our Mailing List

If you would like to be added to our mailing list to receive updates on this and other books, please send your name, address to the above address or sign up on our internet site. Your personal information will never be sold or disclosed.

Contacting the Author

If you have questions or comments for David Daniluk, you may email him at: privatecuisine@greenleafenterprises.com or you may write him at the above address. David welcomes your thoughts and thanks you once again for purchasing this book.